GENTLEMAN OF LEISURE

A YEAR IN THE LIFE OF A PIMP

TEXT BY
Susan Hall

PHOTOGRAPHED BY
Bob Adelman

A SIGNET BOOK
NEW AMERICAN LIBRARY
TIMES MIRROR

To Susan and Peter

SIGNET TRADEMARK REG. U.S. PAT. OFF. AND FOREIGN COUNTRIES
REGISTERED TRADEMARK—MARCA REGISTRADA
HECHO EN CHICAGO, U.S.A.

**SIGNET, SIGNET CLASSICS, SIGNETTE,
MENTOR and PLUME BOOKS**
*are published by The New American Library, Inc.,
1301 Avenue of the Americas, New York, New York 10019*

First Printing, July, 1973

2 3 4 5 6 7 8 9

PRINTED IN THE UNITED STATES OF AMERICA

THIS PIMP MAKES MORE MONEY THAN THE PRESIDENT OF THE UNITED STATES— WHAT DOES HE HAVE THAT MAKES HOOKERS, NORMALLY SO SHREWD WITH MEN, GIVE UP THEIR EARNINGS AND DEVOTE THEMSELVES TO HIM?

"A woman's relationship with a pimp must be selfless. I'm very old-fashioned. It gives me great pleasure to give myself completely to my man."—*Sandy*

"I would like Silky to rape me. Just to pretend. When I asked him, he said, 'How the hell can you rape a bitch whose legs are always open?' "—*Kitty*

"I'd like to have a little Silky, but you shouldn't have a baby when you're a whore."—*Linda*

"Before I met Silky, sex wasn't like this. No man went into all these different positions. Silky comes at you from every side; he's a good lover."—*Tracey*

"A pimp is a father image. His strictness is what you'd expect from a father— he tells you what to do."—*Lois*

GENTLEMAN OF LEISURE—
the mysterious,
private world of a pimp and his women

AUTHOR'S NOTE

Anyone living in a large city has caught fleeting glimpses of flashy men in ornate cars and girls selling themselves on street corners. These are shadowy, underworld figures. In the course of satisfying our curiosity about them, we discovered not stereotypes, but complex people with a defined etiquette, strong passions and even romance.

GENTLEMAN OF LEISURE documents the private life of a pimp and his prostitutes. The people who appear in the photographs are not models. Only names have been changed to protect the "guilty." The text is in their own words.

It is our judgment that, while our subject Silky is more financially successful than most pimps, less violent and perhaps a bit more stylish, the values and attitudes elicited from him and his women are widely shared by pimps and whores and are representative of this way of life.

To our knowledge, this clandestine world has never before been penetrated by camera and tape recorder. At first, we were outsiders and our subjects were mistrustful. When they came to see that we did not judge them, they began to cooperate out of a variety of motives—a feeling that they were misunderstood, a need to confide and justify themselves and also to enhance their own reputations. To our surprise, the subjects liked being photographed, for theirs is a life of display. As in any such effort, a tension exists between the subjects' desire to be placed in a favorable light and the reporters' need for revelation.

Our central concern was the bond that joins a pimp and his women: why a girl voluntarily selects a pimp and stays with him after she has chosen. We wondered what this pimp had that made prostitutes, who are so shrewd with men in their work, give up all their money and dedicate themselves to him. As our knowledge deepened, the question shifted: what was in the prostitutes' predicament that made the pimp seem inevitable.

Using the bond between pimp and whore as our focus, we have woven together bits and pieces of their lives to reveal a very strange love story.

—Susan Hall and Bob Adelman

IDENTIFICATIONS

FALL

SILKY

The term is pimp, but I don't use it, *says Silky*. I'm a professional gentleman of leisure. I have absolutely nothing to do. I stay in bed and take showers. I'm just a connoisseur of resting and a television freak. I do make more money than the President of the United States. If I were in another way of life, I'd have to hustle more. As a black man, I've never had alternatives anyway. I could have played first base, run the mile, or become an entertainer, but I was a natural pimp, so I just pursued my talents.

White society looks down on pimps. They make life hard for us, but they've been doing this to black people for four hundred and thirty-five years, and we've withstood this prejudice, so we must be pretty strong. I've survived and I'm successful, but nobody's helped me. Society doesn't like success in any black person. It's bad enough when you make it, but when you do, they try to take it from you. You're fighting the system all the time, just to maintain your position. Holding on is three-quarters of the job.

I'm having run-ins with the police—over nothing. The cops ask whether my mink coat's real. I say, "No, it's not real." Then they ask how much the diamonds cost. I say, "Ten cents." Cops automatically put pimps down. They think we're all Iceberg Slim. He was an old-time pimp, who worked by force and by the stick. Maybe that type did deserve disrespect. But today, we're more elevated and gentlemanly. Styles have changed in pimping. You don't just leave a girl in a closet for eight hours because she made you mad. Modern pimps use psychiatry.

You can't force a girl into this situation. The girls are not slaves. My girls decide to share my life themselves. It's their decision. A girl might leave and I might go get her. But usually I'm real, show her my charming self, and she choses to stay.

3

There is no game on either side. Most men lie to their wives and have other women. I know, because I get the fifty or a hundred bucks they spend for one of my girls. Most men just give their women lollipops and that's that. The men give my girls lollipops and I end up with the lollipops. I'm completely honest with my women. They know who I see and when, why, and where.

That makes me very different from other men. I've learned to control a woman. Other men are tricks. They'll be driving along and see a cute little piece of ass on the corner. They can't resist, stop, and pay her money. But she gives the money to me, because I am the master. I cannot be tricked. Just the fact that I can dominate women makes other men jealous and afraid of me. Most men let women rule the roost. Maybe that's why they hate pimps.

It used to be, when a pimp came into a black night spot, they'd put the spotlight on him and order drinks on the house. He was respected. Now there's a new trend of jealousy among black men too. You go into a joint and everyone will freeze you. With players, pimps, hustlers, and college students—anyone who's succeeded from the black community—there's an automatic jealousy. Even with barbers. I go to the barber and pay thirty dollars to have my hair done. That barber hates me, because I can afford thirty dollars (even though it's money in his mouth). I've known barbers who left the chair and tried to pimp but wasn't able to. They had to go back to the scissors. You have to have talent in any profession.

The first job I have is copping—getting new girls. I work on new girls all the time. That way, I can pick them, instead of them picking me.

I meet girls at parties, at clubs and after-hour spots, and through my own girls. I can always tell a professional girl. The police can too. They can tell pimps from square guys. They can tell square girls from prostitutes. Our profession involves something different, which you can sense. I could see a girl shopping with curlers in her hair and still tell she was a working girl. I can't explain exactly what it is.

It's almost inevitable that a prostitute ends up with a player. It's hand and glove. Birds of feather. The two just go together. Their heads are in the same place. We have the same thought patterns about life. We live the same life. Most girls look at everyone besides pimps as tricks. Some people think that pimps are whores because they take money, and that whores are tricks because they pay the pimps. It's true that without money a girl can't be mine, no way. A date can't have her unless he pays her.

4

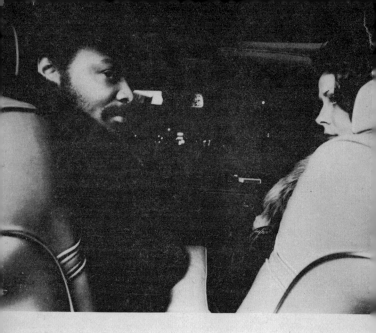

That is a similarity. But the relationship between a pimp and a whore is also a man-woman relationship. It isn't just money. Our personal relationship is number one. Money is a part of that relationship, because money is a rule and a law of the life.

A girl who is a prostitute becomes good at manipulating men. Because I am aware, I don't allow her to manipulate me. With me, she has the one relationship that isn't a "use" relationship. She needs a pimp for her personal life. He's the only one who can understand, appreciate, *and* handle her.

When I go copping—to tote that barge and lift that bale—I be myself and go out. I look anywhere and everywhere for girls—straight or not. That makes no difference. If I catch someone that's already in the life, great. It's a short cut. But I also have the gift of converting. I turn girls out.

A few weeks ago I went to Montreal. I met Sherry. She was working for the phone company and was in a little pub for college people. I'm natural. I don't think everytime I meet a girl "How come she might want me?" I have grown through experience. Little itty-bitty things accumulate. Like Sherry had continued to go to the ladies' room just to walk by me at the bar. I knew she was attracted. I could utilize that.

Sherry handed me her matches when she wanted a light. A

stranger can't do that to me, and my woman wouldn't. I knew Sherry didn't want to have her way. Most men would let her. A straight girl would make her man get the laundry and clean up the kitchen. If he'll let her, she'll give him no other choice. She'll be boss. But I don't feel any woman wants to be boss. I won't let her. Women like to be dominated.

Finally, Sherry got around to asking what I did. I said I was a gentleman of leisure. She didn't understand. She said, "Is that a pimp?" I said, "In a sense. But it's a graduated version. A Ph.D. in pimping." She gave me her phone number, and a couple of days later I called.

We went out and I explained things to her. I don't have a script. I just try to make myself important to her. The only way she can be with me is my way. When I feel she's swept, I make my points. Women are drawn to me sexually, but I purposely try to underplay sex. If the relationship begins on sex, that's the only way I can keep a girl. I have to service her. If the relationship begins with me personally, then I can keep her with my charming personality. We begin to like each other. If she likes me well enough, she'll do anything. Sherry was supposed to come to New York and she never showed. I guess I struck out that time. If I meet her again, we'll talk and laugh, but there won't be anything personal between us. We won't go see *The Great White Hope*.

I hope the situation comes up where a girl enjoys my company and I enjoy hers. This is my way of life, and I'd like her to join it. There's no trickery on my part. I met a girl at a party the other night. She had a guy in California and he brought her here. I don't know what he told her, but it must have been lies, because she was very unhappy and confused. Now we enjoyed talking and being together on this one particular evening. We came home and stayed together. There was something personal going between us. There has to be, because I ask her to gamble her life for me. She takes an oath to dedicate herself to me. I'm a pimp and she's got to go out, work, and bring me money. It's that simple.

Now this girl is working with my best ladies. She's being trained to follow their mannerisms. I don't have anything to do with the ladies' business. I couldn't tell them how to turn a date, 'cause I've never turned one. I couldn't tell them what to say, 'cause I've never been on the set. I have no affiliation with their business and very, very seldom is it ever discussed. It's not that I don't care, but I certainly don't want to seem like a little freak—always wanting to hear what happened. Knowing their business would also be work for me and I don't work.

It used to be the only way a girl was accepted by a pimp was when she brought him money—like a dowry. That's going out of fashion. Now a girl wants to be around you a bit before she gets involved. She wants to see your style and your way of living. This is the modern girl.

Most of the girls I meet come and go. That's where the pimping comes in. I always start a girl with the hope that she will stay forever. But if I begin to sense that she won't, because she's flaky or immature, then I try to get as much money as I can before she blows. If she has sixty days, I try to get six thousand dollars out of her. Then she can go about her business.

Girls usually run off over silly things. Like, I say I'll take her out on Friday. On Friday, I don't. So she runs off. She phones and says I broke a promise. But what promise? I just forgot. I'm human. I might have had an accident and be in the hospital. That doesn't make any difference. "You promised, superman."

If a girl is interested in building a life with me, then I can make an investment in her and give her a foundation. She gets an apartment and presents on her birthday, Christmas, and our anniversary. The relationship builds.

I'm not extra romantic. I just don't say, "I love you." Every woman might love me and feel that I love her. I don't feel as strongly about my ladies as they feel about me. I'm not a woman. If my emotions got the best of me, if I couldn't control myself, it would be dangerous. I must treat all my girls equally and with cool. I've got to control *them*.

After we've been together for a year or so, a dedication is built. Loyalty and understanding creates a kind of love in me. It becomes complete man-woman.

There's another kind of love—seeing somebody who's beautiful and being swept. I can't afford that.

The average pimp has two girls. One would be less difficult. But two is a challenge to the male and the girls. To make a woman sell herself is quite a task. To ask her to share her man is even more difficult. With two girls, sharing is very obvious. But if a girl comes to me now, and I have seven or eight women, she couldn't possibly be jealous or complain to me, because she knew all about my women before she came on board. One-eighth of me is not too much, but the girls are satisfied. That is my talent.

There are things I can't do, regardless, as a professional. I cannot take up with a square girl. It wouldn't be fair. My girls are out in thirty-degree weather, working and earning money for me. I can't sit home, warm, and in the company of a straight

8

lady. There are some women who would sacrifice me not to get into this business. One girl who I was engaged to, and who had my only child, cares more for me than anyone I've ever met. But she would not be a prostitute for me. I don't care what proposition I would make, or how much I'd promise her, she would not go to work. She lives in the Bronx. She can't afford a telephone. But she wouldn't walk the streets for anything in the world.

For me to take up with a square girl would be disrespecting my girls. This is a code I honor. If I had women around who didn't work, why would the others have to? My girl Sandy doesn't like the business. The only reason she works is for me. Sandy shows no jealousy, but she's a woman. For me to mess with square girls would put her out. And it would put my status down. It would be simping, not pimping. Simping is half-assed pimping.

Fortunately, I have very attractive women for myself, so I seldom even think about a woman who isn't with me. I feel very strongly for my girls. They make a large sacrifice for me and I appreciate their dedication. If the situation were reversed and I were a woman, I wouldn't do this for anything in the world. So there's real admiration on my part.

Now I don't have anything but white girls. I've had black girls all my life, but it's rough with them. Black women have a harder time getting dates; they have a harder time with the police, and a harder time with society. They don't necessarily make half the money of a white girl, but they only get half a chance to make the money.

All blacks—me included—have an inner, hidden pain. Some overcome it; some never do. We have it because we're black and we've been put in a certain underdog category. That put-down is around you every minute of your life.

Black women don't get along with each other. White women decide that they're in this situation and they're going to make the best of it. With blacks, a hidden larceny comes out. They say little things to hurt each other. It's weird and it's rough.

At times I've had both black and white women and it was a total mess. The black girl felt persecuted and attacked her wife-in-law. For a professional like me, white women are better. They can make more money, they're more tolerant of my other women, and the ship sails smoothly.

To me, there's not much difference between white and black women except color. With the lights off, there isn't any difference. I like them both in bed. But the blacks have always been in a difficult situation, and they can't stop testing me with cracks and obvious arguments. Two white women will not argue in front of me. They're not as competitive as blacks. Oh, they might compete in making me a chili—they'll try to out-cook each other. But white women concentrate on pleasing me and making me happy.

I sincerely try to have a personal relationship with every girl. If we continue to be together, we progress. I try to make ladies out of my women. I train them. I give them my style. They're to please me. I never have to speak more than once.

Sex plays a part in our relationship, but it is not the main part. Casanova is dead. And Rudolph. The great lovers aren't in fashion. If I allowed sex to become important, pimping would be a job for me. I'd become a sex machine with eight women. Instead, I emphasize the emotional aspect and the development of our personal and social relationship. My women really enjoy my masculinity. They enjoy being controlled and directed.

Not many men are capable of being completely in charge. I am. If a woman complains, I do not respond in a sympathetic fashion. I treat her like a child. I might even beat her up a bit. It gives me no pleasure, but sometimes it works. I'm not a beater-upper. I do a lot of hollering. Really we should be able to discuss a problem and eliminate it. But if she acts like a child, I have to treat her like one. I have to be a man—three hundred sixty degrees.

I try to have unison and harmony. A woman has to be very mature to make this adjustment. When she first chooses me, she might be a little girl. But to progress in our relationship, she must become personally mature as a woman.

I control all my girls. It's like being President of the United States. If the President makes a move, we must back him, even if he's in error. I'm in the same position. If I make a move—right or wrong—the girls must back me. I do make mistakes, but they've got to stand by them. I am not a dictator. My bottom woman, Sandy—she's been with me longest—takes care of most of my business and helps me make decisions. She's earned that position.

She oversees all my expenses, which are very high. I have a tremendous overhead. Apartment rents alone are thirty-seven hundred a month. The phone bills are ridiculous. The phone company keeps sending bigger and bigger bills. The girls call their parents and their friends. They have a mental thing about how large they are. "The phone bill ain't nothing." They talk to Suzy in Nova Scotia for two hours. I don't know this specifically, because I don't check the bills. If there was a bill a girl

thought would make me angry, she would say the phone bill was two hundred and put in fifty herself. It would never get back to me.

I have to change my phone number all the time. Sandy called me from Puerto Rico and she paid for every call herself. But for some reason they charged me for all those calls. My bill was five hundred ninety-seven dollars. So I had to get a new number.

I used to call up and give a black name and say, "Hello dare" in a deep voice. Then Sandy took over. She uses Jewish names. She says, "This is David Goldstein's secretary. I would like a new phone." I used to have to put down big deposits, but since I've been using Jewish names, I ain't paid a penny.

My tools are also very expensive. I'm continually sharpening my cars, my jewelry, and my clothes. These are tools like a policeman has a gun. I'm bettering my position and playing for position—just like a businessman. If I didn't have the jewelry and the cars, I couldn't get the girls I get. I have the best ladies in town. Ladies want to come to a man that's doing something with his money.

Women are attracted to me because I wear my money. I have a certain mannerism and style. I design all my own clothes and they are made to order. I also design my jewelry. To some individuals, I don't look masculine. There's a lady in my building who came to a New Year's party about three years ago. She asked me if I fooled around with fellows. That was her interpretation of a lace shirt and curly hair—we're fags. I never bother to think whether someone will consider me sweet. I'm confident in my masculinity. If I like a garment, I'll add it to my wardrobe. My taste depends on the style I want. I'm about five years ahead of the times. The way you dress is part of the competition in this game. So, may the best man win.

When you buy a car like mine, it is definitely for attention. I am recognized by the bubble. It's me. I have it for myself— personal. I've put about ten thousand dollars into customization. I have a Rolls-Royce grille, alligator-skin roof dyed gold, and the orange bubble. It expresses me. That helps with the girls. My own girls are proud of the car. Other girls, who might one day be mine, notice me driving around and get to know me through the car.

But the car is a nuisance. When I come out of a store, there are dozens of people around it. As a matter of fact, the car's protected by a human alarm system.

Any garage man who sees my car, knows I'm a pimp, thinks I have money, and tries to take me. The car has been in the garage every day for two weeks now. For example, my gas gauge says one-half full and I run out of gas. I call the garage and they come and tow me for twenty dollars. The next day, the car starts smoking. That's another alternator for seventy-five dollars. I called to tell the garage my grille was lose and to be sure and put it up. I'm riding along and think I've run over something in the street. Sure enough it's the grille. I honestly believe people in the garage are doing little things to that car. It's expensive.

The car has served its purpose—at the fights and for special occasions. It's probably helped me get some ladies. But I'm growing out of it. The customizing singles me out for the police.

Almost every day I get hassled. Illegally hassled. Unlawfully hassled. A policeman followed me the other night. He waited till we got out of the car and locked it up before he asked for the registration. His obvious purpose was to make us stand in the cold. I am a professional and I didn't argue with him in any way. I talk to him nice and say, "Officer, there's some kind of mistake." But he goes on talking to me nasty when he sees I'm not militant. If you go cussing and acting crazy, then you don't get no hassle out of a policeman. He gets nervous, pulls out his

12

pistol, and hurries up and gets away. But not without some nasty remarks like, "Where'd you get that coat?" I mean, for real. He'll say, "Do you screw her?" pointing to a girl. The police are jealous of pimps, because we have white women and money. But don't think the cops don't cost me too.

My girls were counting salaries—the salaries that each of the girls make and the salary I make. What they consider my salary is the money I've made all year from girls who cop and blow— they just come and go. I've made two hundred thousand in the past seven months by myself. That's twenty-six girls. My regulars—who I've copped and locked—that's Sandy and Kitty and Linda—they each made around seventy-five thousand last year.

Each girl gives me all the money she makes. In turn, I give her a place to stay—her own apartment if she's been with me for a while, I pay her bail, and she has ten dollars a day expense money. I'm very casual about collecting. Most fellows collect immediately because they have no trust and no confidence. When I first started, I had to have my money yesterday. I've outgrown that.

I used to drive around and watch the girls. A lot of fellows try to keep their girls in check. Occasionally, I'll drive around to see if there's an unhappy lady who belongs to another fellow. You can get girls that way. You invite them to breakfast, and if they're impressed or sad, they might say yes. But checking my own—I have too much respect for them. I know they give me all their money. My girls would not stash. Money's not that important. It's just necessary and part of living in the world as well as we do.

Of course, with girls I really like, I'd prefer they didn't have to see dates. I'd prefer that none of us had to do anything. That would be great. But we need money. I don't think a girl is hurt by being a prostitute. The human mind can adjust to anything. Being a prostitute is acting. The girl turns her mind and her feelings off. It's a job. She portrays making love. She can't wait to get off that job. But I don't think it does any damage. I'm all the more important to her, because, when she gets with me, she can let herself go. She don't show her real self to tricks.

I've never had a girl who really liked her work. Some girls just drift into the life; others need money. But once they've started, it's hard to be without a man. Particularly if the girl is on the street. I provide a relationship, fun and understanding. I *know* their work is hard.

Pimping itself is mentally hard. Everything you're doing is with yourself and for yourself. You have no one to answer to

except yourself. You make a mistake and it's against yourself. I'm running my own business. I'm the president and the whole corporation.

I am selfish. Silky likes Silky. Silky only thinks about Silky. Some women get satisfaction out of pleasing a man. That's the kind of woman for me. I have confidence in myself. I feel that any girl of intelligence will accept this life and her position in it. Myself—I like cutie pies—attractive young girls. It is not necessary for an attractive young girl to enter this life. She could sit on her butt and enjoy the comforts of any man. But for her to stop whatever she's doing and dedicate her life to me makes all the difference in the world. A girl makes a sacrifice for me. The only greater sacrifice would be for her to jump out a window. A girl gives up her home, her relationship with her family. I become her whole life. That means our relationship is more passionate and romantic than most.

I don't know of any place where you can make as much money as fast. This entire movement is a short cut for me. If I were in any other profession, I could not be where I am now—at this early age of twenty-five. The life is a short cut to the moon. I want what Howard Hughes has had for years. Complete and total success. Security and all. Not just one or two shots at being secure. Owning half of New York. Being sincerely rich.

It seems as though I've been pimping all my life. When I was a baby, I didn't know it had a name. I used to bring two or three girl friends home at once. I lived with my mother and grandmother. At six, having several girl friends didn't seem peculiar. But I've continued to do this. When my mother realized I was a pimp, she asked me to get a job and settle down with one girl. Society bans pimping and my mother is a member of society. I'm breaking the law and she wanted me to be a doctor, a lawyer, or an Indian chief. I still think I'd make a great Indian chief. Maybe I'll do that when I retire.

At fourteen, I started going to the Music Box at night. You wasn't supposed to go there till you were twenty-one. My grandmother went to sleep about nine and my mother left at eleven every night to gamble. I'd slip out. One night, I got busted at the Box. They called my mother and she came down with my father. I hadn't seen him for a year. I was standing by the bar and backed out when I seen them coming.

My father was always my hero. He never helped me in any way, but he was my favorite. Every time he came by, my mother became secondary. Here's daddy. I haven't seen him for six months and I was so glad to see him, I put my mother aside. I hurt her. I can see it in her eyes today. But when daddy came, I'd stop everything for the five hours he'd be home.

From what I've heard since I've been grown, my father tried to pimp and that's what broke up his relationship with my mother.

When I first started pimping successfully, I came home with my new Eldorado. My father's attitude turned me against him. I didn't understand. He looked at me like he wished I would run the car into the wall and crash it right fast. I said, "Dad. Look. This is a 1969 brand-new Eldorado. And I put five thousand down in cash."

He said, "Yeh. That's nice."

I'd say, "Let's run over to Uncle Charlie's or Uncle Herbie's."

And he'd say "I've got something to do. Call me again before you leave." Just like that.

My stepsister said, "Daddy told me about the car. Baby, he's so jealous it's a shame. It's really sick."

Actually, the first time I knocked off a woman, I went and told my father. I said, "I don't know what to do, but I have to go and tell this girl's fellow that she's chosen me. I'd like you to be with me when I go.

He said, "Cool, if that's the way you feel about it."

My father went with me and stood by while I explained. After that, we got high. I never knew he smoked reefers. We've smoked once or twice again.

Later, when I went home before the Muhammad Ali fight, Dad said, "Move over. I'm going to drive that car of yours." And while we were driving, he told me, "This is the hardest profession to do well in and I'd hate to see you jam up in the middle and have to start all over again when you're forty." He never did get no place as a pimp.

When I was in junior high school, my family moved to Shaker Heights—a middle-class neighborhood that was way over our heads. All the little girls had money, and I didn't even have to ask them for it. They'd just give me money and I began to expect it. I'd go out with girls who were a little older than me, and if we were going to a party or a special occasion, we'd go downtown and buy twin outfits. The girl would pay.

I got sent to a correctional institution—a school for bad boys —because I was picked up on an illegal entry charge. Some older guys had thrown a brick through a window and we saw them. A couple of hours later, we came back and they hadn't got up the nerve to go in the store, so we did. We got caught. When the police came, we were arguing over what to take. I was interested in a tape recorder. But I really wasn't a delinquent kid.

The minimum in an institution is nine months, but the superintendent and the supervisor got behind me and I only stayed for four. While I was there I was a track star, and Kent State—which was big in track—offered me a scholarship. I intended to take it, but I lost my interest in education. If I'd continued with my schooling, I'd be educated and hungry right now. Instead, I make more money than the President and I haven't even begun in this life.

But I wouldn't suggest that any man quit what he's doing and try this. It's you against the world. The girls ain't every day. All of them could run off tonight and where would I be. Right where I started from. With nothing.

I always loved entertainment and began singing with a group. One fellow was supposed to be drafted and leave the group and I was going to take his place. But then he went back to his wife and they couldn't draft him. Meanwhile, they introduced me to another group and I joined them.

That group went at it all wrong. They made it so hard. They'd just rehearse and rehearse. I had girls and they requested that I not have girls. I'd just bought a new Buick and it had notes of one hundred ninety dollars a month on it. I couldn't afford that car without girls. To keep on singing would mean to give up the Buick. So I gave up singing entirely. I just stayed with my girls and dedicated myself to the profession.

If you keep on doing something year after year, you're bound to grow up and learn the tricks of your trade. I'm twenty-five and I've been a professional for nine years. I'd been pimping before that, but I didn't know what I was doing, so I wouldn't call me a pimp. I'd have girls on the corner in front of the county courthouse. At eighteen, I got my first professional lady. She showed me where the stroll was in town. Then I realized that other fellows were doing it too. Up till then, I figured it all out for myself. I was a young whippersnapper, running around hollering what I had in mind to do. Then I began to pimp seriously and put my girls on the stroll.

I'd go to Akron—which was a smaller town—and work my girls there until I felt they were ready for the big city of Cleveland. Even while I was in school, I'd take off on the road with two girls as soon as summer vacation came. In September, I'd be right back in school.

When I graduated, I just traveled from town to town for a few years. Then I decided to settle and make it in the Big Apple. New York is the toughest town to work in, but it's also the most rewarding financially.

A DAY IN SILKY'S LIFE

Silky: I'm going to make some knickers. I've got boots that will come up to midcalf. I've got great legs that I've been concealing all these years. [He laughs at himself]

Tailor: No problem. No problem.

Silky: I want a whole suit out of this material. But I don't want no pockets.

Tailor: Let me write that down. It's a beautiful piece of material. Want all five suits the same?

Silky: These two I want just plain. With one button. The others will be knickers. I'm going to be a giant.

Tailor: You want the flap in the patch pocket and the pleat?

Silky: Okay. And one with bell bottoms.

Tailor: You didn't tell me about these jackets. Big collar and lapels?

Silky: And a flap over the pockets.

Tailor: But no top buttons. One button. Single-breasted.

Silky: Pleat in the back. How about cuffs?

Tailor: Let's try them. If you don't like them we can always take them off.

Silky: I'm thinking about getting a Rolls-Royce. Going to be a giant.

Tailor: They don't make better cars. They're lifetime cars. I know a fellow who bought one for twenty-five thousand and drove it down to his home in Alabama. People said, "He must be doing bad up in New York. An old car like that."

Silky: I've been wearing my coats long. Let's make them shorter.

Tailor: I'll take measurements. As far as I can calculate, you have five suits and two extra pairs of pants. That's seven hun-

dred dollars. I didn't charge you no tax on it. Everything will be ready next weekend. I'll call.

George: I put oil over my skin to keep it from drying.

Silky: I'm sweating.

George: This is the only time you work up a sweat, Silky.

Silky: Oh, sometimes I do when I get down on a girl. Then I raise some sweat and need a little Kentucky fried chicken for energy.

George: How do you satisfy seven women sexually—are you a nympho? How many times a day do you have sex?

Silky: Not a day. A week. I don't have it every day.

George: I don't believe you.

Silky: What do you think I am? Hercules?

George: I think you must have sex every day.

Silky: What do you think I am, Ben Hur? If you had a bowl full of apples, would you eat apples every day?

George: No. But I might eat cherries.

Silky: I have sex four or five times a week.

George: Well, I guess you can satisfy a woman just laying there beside her. I know one girl who comes just holding me. Or biting me. Maybe she's a freak. But seven girls. That's one I have to figure out for myself. I've had trouble enough with three girl friends at once.

Silky: I purposely don't have sex every day. I have too many women. I'm not having sex with the same woman. I'm having it with different women. Some girls haven't had sex for five days. Those girls are going to be really serious [laughing].

George: The other day I said, and you denied it, in order to be a pimp, you've got to be a freak.

Silky: There's a freak in everybody.

George: Do you have your girls sucking on you every time you have sex? Most girls like that. But it takes a lot out of you. When you discharge in regular sex, they say you lose a drop and a half of blood. When a girl sucks you off, you lose two drops of blood.

Silky: You can give a quart and it don't do nothing to you. You're talking about drops.

George: I believe in preserving my health. With your girls, you hold things together on the strength of your joint and not your brain.

Silky: Well, I hold the relationships together. I'm proud of that.

George: I heard that two of your women were laying each other.

Silky: I don't think that any of my girls like girls. I haven't

21

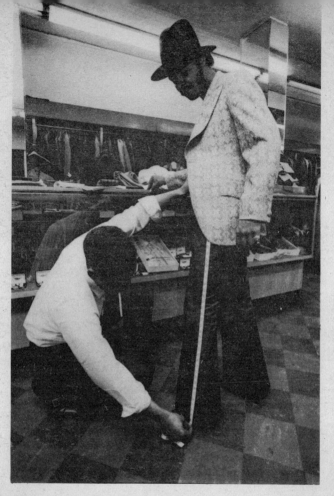

heard any rumors. I have no reason to think so—with the possible exception of Kitty. I am so much against it and my girls know it. I speak on it all the time and get excited. I won't have it around me.

George: If a person is bisexual, it's hard to tell. Only the people they want to know, know. If a girl is lonely and she doesn't see you often, a relationship with a girl might be perfect.

Silky: If you and I were making it—it's the same parable as far as I'm concerned.

George: Not as far as I'm concerned.

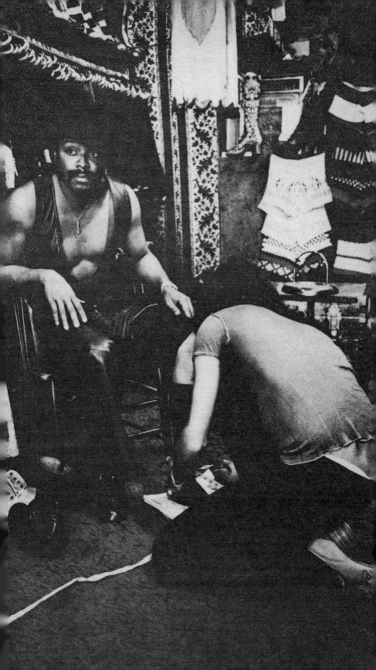

Silky: Coming home and catching me in your arms—coming home and catching her in her arms.

George: I regard it as helping you with your homework. A woman who's qualified to do that, she could be number one on your list.

Silky: It would be the end of our relationship. I don't like it.

Silky: You're late!

Sandy: It's been three weeks since I seen you. Why don't we cook in my backyard?

Silky: You girls get everything!

Sandy: [Teasing] I wouldn't say you wore nothing on your wrist.

Silky: Tonight I'm going on the town incognito.

Sandy: How're you going to do that? "Iceberg Slim." They always say, "There goes Iceberg Slim" when you're out with me.

Silky: You look bad tonight.

Sandy: So do you. Really bad. I ended up at the beauty parlor at six o'clock.

Silky: I know you. I knew you were late 'cause you just had to have your hair done before our date.

Sandy: You should have seen the cute little boy that was at the beauty shop with his mother. He had on a real diamond watch with a ring to match. The hairdresser said, "What do you want to be when you grow up?"

The boy said, "A pimp. My daddy's a pimp." Everyone in the shop said by the time he's sixteen he'll have a penthouse.

26

Silky: Or a backyard! . . . How're we going to celebrate?

Sandy: Get stoned. Want a smoke? It's good grass.

Silky: I've been smoking so much it doesn't make me feel high. It makes me calm. Slows me down. I have a tendency to move fast.

Sandy: [Sarcastic] Not in my direction! But you do sing good.

Silky: Some guy uptown wants me to write songs.

Sandy: With your sense of humor!

Silky: If I wrote, "Mary had a little lamb, one, two," it would be a hit.

Sandy: But now songs are involved with real life. It's not a lamb any more. It's based on "Mary had a pimp."

Silky: That's how I can do it. For real. . . . Hey. Did you hear the joke about the priest and the hooker? [Sandy doesn't respond] That's supposed to be the joke.

Sandy: That's the corniest joke I ever, ever heard. Believe it or not, I have a priest as a trick. He takes off his collar before he comes in the door. Then he says, "Sandy, you're the wickedest person I know."

I says, "You must be wicked too. You *come* here." We laugh and fuck. This happens every time.

Silky: You talk to Linda* today?

Sandy: I never do. Hardly ever.

Silky: I've been having trouble with her. She's in love with herself.

*One of Silky's wives.

Sandy: I think everyone's in love with themselves.

Silky: But this is an over-added amount.

Sandy: She's distant to me.

Silky: I say she's a bitch. She has no business to challenge me to see how I'll react. She didn't want me to see you. She wanted me to see her. I see her every day. You—well, it's been almost a month—'cause I can count on you, baby. But Linda challenged me and tried to get more attention and more action. She has no sympathy for the fact that I have five women. She's on a solo flight. Sometimes I think she forgets she has to work to be with me. She doesn't like the *word* prostitute.

Sandy: Once she said she was going to choose Flash. She thought she'd make you real, real jealous, 'cause he's your biggest competition.

Silky: Flash is an old man now. He can't step with me. Let her choose.

Sandy: Well, I don't think she'd choose anyway. 'Cause she told me she couldn't even remember what Flash looked like!

Silky: I think I can make Linda a good woman. She has it in her. She's sure in love with me. But I've got to work hard to put the whore in her.

Sandy: I'll tell you something funny about whores. The woman sitting next to me in the beauty parlor said, "Don't give me that red nail polish. Only *whores* wear that. My manicurist laughed, because she knows what I do. So when she starts to do my nails, I says, "Don't give me that red nail polish. I may be a whore, but I don't like that red." The woman gasped.

I said, "You should always be careful, 'cause you don't know who you're sitting next to."

Kitty got Jesus and Terry back today. Hear about it?

Silky: No. Sometimes I just don't want to hear what Kitty's up to.

Sandy: Well, this is one story that will make you laugh. Terry had made about two thousand dollars in the past week and a half. Jesus kept promising her she could go shopping and Terry was counting on it. But Jesus gambles. He's always coming home with no money. He has two other girls and don't ever see Terry no more.

Now Terry's real hurt, 'cause they've been together for years, right? Grew up in the same home town. He had his eyes on her from the time she was nine years old. He actually kept her for two years before he turned her out. So they're real close.

Terry has this two hundred fifty dollars and Kitty tells her to go shopping. Terry calls Jesus and says she wants to see him. He says, "You're not going to tell me what to do."

29

And she says, "I'm going shopping."

Jesus says, "You don't say what you want to do. You just do what I tell you. Anyway, your money can't buy what I want and it can't buy *me* for you." He slammed down the phone. Terry tries to call him back and he won't answer.

So Kitty cooks up this big story to get them to make up. She calls Jesus and says, "I just want you to know that I don't want to get into your business."

He says, "Yeah."

Kitty says, "But Jesus, Terry is going crazy. I don't know how to explain this, but she called me up and she's laughing and screaming and crying. She came over to my apartment and starts burning up her money." Kitty knew this would get Jesus. She actually did burn a dollar bill to make it real.

So Kitty says to Jesus, "I snatched the money away from her. I asked her what the hell she was doing. Then Terry says, 'Jesus don't want me no more. He don't even want my money.'" Kitty tells Jesus she finally calmed her down, but she says to Jesus, "Terry doesn't think you want her."

Jesus says, "Is Terry with you now?"

Kitty says, "Her coat's still here so she couldn't have gone too far because it's raining outside."

Jesus tells Kitty to hold on to Terry if she comes back and that he'll be over in a minute. Now all the time Terry is standing in the room. Kitty tells her to play it off like she's ready to commit suicide.

So when Jesus knocks on the door, Kitty sends Terry into the bathroom and tells her to lock the door from the inside and start running the bathwater and screaming. Jesus comes in and says, "Where is she?"

You know how great Kitty is at putting on an act. She says,

"Can't you hear her, Jesus. She's locked in the bathroom with the water running and there's razor blades inside."

Jesus gets really panicked. He bangs on the door. Terry won't answer. He begs. He pleads. He promises her she can go shopping. He promises her she don't have to work so hard. He promises to spend more time with her. All the time, Terry's crying and screaming. In the middle of all this, Kitty shows Jesus the burned dollar bill and says hundreds of them were just flushed down the toilet.

Finally Jesus says if Terry will come out, he'll send her to a psychiatrist to help her out. Terry makes him promise. She don't want to go to no doctor, but she does want Jesus and she wants him to pay attention to her. Maybe because of Kitty, he'll see her for a while.

Kitty says she's going shopping too, so be careful. Kitty's a shoe freak, you know.

Silky: Well, if there's one thing you have to have on the street, it's shoes! . . . Could you use some smothered chicken? Let's go.

DANDY

I've been knowing Dandy since I was in elementary school, *Silky recalls*. He taught me to cross on the green, not in between. I was a pimp before I knew he was one. I thought he played cards or hustled or played craps. He always had money. I was just a kid.

Dandy is one of the few people that's seen me all the way. We've had our little outs, but it's probably because we're both professionals. We stay the best of friends.

In order to be a citizen of the United States—a reputable citizen—you must hold a position, *Dandy says*. Jobwise. Familywise. Imagine me—twelve or thirteen years ago in the ghetto. Any chick I could have. Visualize me picking from all them chicks—one. To sit off on top of the hill with a little white house and a picket fence. Me sitting in a rocking chair with babies running around all day.

But nobody wants to be enclosed. You could be a vagabond and be here, there, and everywhere—a gigolo. But you don't build and you end up with nothing. To make a success, you have to pursue a career. At the time they brought Dandy on this earth, there was very little a man could do to bring himself up out of the ghetto. If my father had gone to college, he still couldn't have gotten a job. The only way for him to get out of the ghetto was to pimp.

I got pride in the profession from my dad. He pimped a little and was always around the life. He said, "Be the best and don't settle for less. Be a sweet mack. Be a successful man."

Young fellows start practicing very young. Pimps can manipulate. They can figure out a problem and its solution, where the average man is so caught up in the process he just sees things the way they are. He doesn't look for the truth. Very early, some mother's son is out practicing on some mother's daughter. But two and two won't do. You have to hustle. So you get a girl friend—you're courting each other in junior high school—and you go off to the basement and get you a piece. When you get through school, you don't have any alternatives. Play a little baseball, play a little basketball, or play a little game with mama's daughter. So you go to telling her, "I saw a guy the other day and he sure had a pretty car. Let's stand on the corner and see if he comes by." Then you both look up and see this fellow—sharp, and his girl's sharp.

Next time you go to a weekend dance where everybody will be, you want to be as sharp as that fellow and his girl. So your chick either has to steal some popsicle sticks, get deposits from pop bottles, save her lunch money, or go out on the stroll. That's the way to start. Because in the ghetto, every teen-age kid wants to be sharp. Our whole people love clothes. It's a sense of taste and style. By being deprived for so long, we grab at an opportunity not to be deprived. Everyone's down for being better and best. This is self-pride. It's not simply pride in the profession I've chosen. It's a pride in being black and being best.

Coming up, you hear tales of pimps. Great pimps who never lose nothing. Great pimps who lose everything and come back. I was the protégé of a pimp who was sixty-eight years old. I lived with him and worked side by side with him every day. We'd get up and get dressed and go and look for women. He'd tell me when things would come out of my mouth that wasn't cool, that wasn't devastating or penetrating to a woman. You have to say words that will stick to her brain and mean something to her, he'd tell me.

A fellow, Scatterbrain, impressed me. He had so many girls and so many cars. He was one of the first fellows to buy a car you could turn into a boat and ride right out into the water. He then went into the Mafia and Cosa Nostra, did drug transactions and slot machines and pin-ball machines and his own barbecues. Finally he got into buying buildings. A lot of successful men in my town used to have women and built themselves through women.

There was Barry Williams. Every year he had a brand-new Eldorado and a brand new Rolls-Royce. The first day they hit the street, he'd be right in front of the barbershop. I'd watch him jumping off yachts and into his penthouse. And I'd watch him change his crop. Just like farmers, pimps change their crops. The girls get stalemated, arrogant, or distrustful. As well as I'm in love and appreciate a woman for being in love with me, I could just as soon let her go off in the wild blue yonder and never look her way again. I have great confidence in me. I

know that somewhere in town there's a woman that's going to dance to *my* music.

I also know of pimps that landed up in the penitentiary. One fellow didn't have nothing but white women. Some of the rich mothers of the girls got charges against him. He fought his own case in court. He was brilliant and intelligent and sharp about what's going on. But he lost his case, did time, and was sentenced to a mental institution. He's being held in jail right now. That's everything I wouldn't want to be.

For him, it was reverse slavery. He didn't take it out on his black sisters. He took his grievances out on white women who were his white slaves. That's what they got him for—white slavery. He was successful, but he was a damn fool. He was headstrong and thought he could handle the system without a lawyer's help. My lawyers are around all the time.

Women have always carried the weight. It's a woman's place to carry the burden. Japanese woman do everything. Throughout time, the great women have been at the top of kingdoms. A lot of my work is sold on the basis of what happened in history during the B.C.'s Salome. Cleopatra. Eve. Helen of Troy. Now some women just want to make money and be right by their man—the man that's being right by them. But a woman can only be as great as her man. Some men are satisfied with a little of this or a little of that. Just as long as they're impersonating another great mack. "I've seen Huckleberry Finn with ten carats on his chest, so I'll get me three and be just as great." Goes like that. If Silky's mind was stagnating and he didn't think to greater lengths and extremes, Sandy wouldn't think to greater lengths and extremes. If a pimp's mind was staying on the sixth floor overlooking the Grand Union grocery store, his woman wouldn't be dreaming of penthouses. A pimp must put that idea in motion.

I have to make the headlines all the time. A year ago, I was in the workhouse for a misdemeanor—traffic tickets. A slow moment in my life. My woman told me she had some money she didn't have. I told her to bring it to the workhouse and put it on the book for me. She said she'd bring it Sunday. I didn't trust her no ways, but she was all I had.

She didn't come. So on Monday, I broke out of the workhouse—we had a secret way of getting in and out. I went home and kicked her ass. I chastised her. They had it going all over town: "A bitch ain't safe even when her man's in jail. Dandy came home and kicked his woman's ass." Imagine me coming

38

out of the workhouse in workhouse drag and putting my finger in a pross's face and saying, "Girl, where is my money? What have you been doing? Do you think just because I'm in the workhouse you can do whatever you want to do on me?" These people who are kicking you around and pushing your name—it helps you. It gives you a rep.

In Cleveland, a good player is talked about over the coffee cups. He means money to the community, because he spends money. If he's elite and gentlemanly, he's nice to be around and you enjoy his company. So mothers talk about players over coffee:

"They tell me Dandy was in the speakeasy last night throwing champagne bottles at the wall."

"Oh, he was?"

"Yes, having fun."

If I'm doing good and I got a smile on my face from ear to ear and my pocket is chugged, if I'm mentally sharp and they can't get a word in edgewise, they say, "Goddamn, Dandy's selling. He's doing well."

Pimps are discriminated against all the time. One night I was out with a fellow and we saw a girl walking down Broadway. She'd been drinking and we tried to pick her up. At that moment, a 1971 Eldorado pulls up to the curb and some guys started kicking the car. One fellow gets out and they knock him down, his head is bleeding, and he's lying on the curb.

The police come by and try to blame me. I thought I was going to get charged for murder. They hauled me down to jail and they wasn't being rough, but they tried to provoke me. They talked like the fellow was dead and said I'd done it. "You pimps always do things like that." I got shaken up.

I went into a deep conversation with the police. I felt that they jumped to conclusions and harassed people. Just because I'm a gentleman of leisure, they pressure me more. I told them there were good fellows and bad and they should be more of a judge. Not just a judge of who is and who isn't a pimp. But a judge of who's good and who's bad among pimps. Some pimps do slam people against the wall. But you *can* be an elevated, cultivated pimp.

The game is deep. In being a mack, you're supposedly the supreme being of man. Man rules woman. In being a mack, you acknowledge this fact. You put yourself in a superior position and you don't let a woman put you in no position. Most women are very tricky. They like to have their own way. But "women of the night" don't look up to a man they can do anyway they want to. He's a john then. Just a trick.

A mack is strong and dominant as well as understanding women. A man must let his wife know that he controls her. But it's even more important for a player. His women encounter all kinds of men and for them to have one man, he must be dominant and make her strong. If you get a weak pross, she's going to be handled by the johns. They'll *use* her. You know how inadequate a woman can be. You've got to instill larceny and trickery to the woman. She can't be shaky and flaky and easily led astray. When her man says, "Woman, do this," it will be done. You're a man running a household. You're also a little bit of God and Jesus. Everything I tell my women, they must do. If I tell my woman to do something and she hesitates, I'm mad.

With a black woman, I become her man. The white man has always made the black man look like a boy. He never got a chance to express his manhood. If he did, people said he was a fool or a trouble maker. The black woman took all the responsibilities. Her man would make a lot of babies and run. So the black woman didn't have no man but me. I'd teach her to conduct herself and to maintain her femininity. Women like a man who dominates, because then they don't lose their womanhood. That's an advantage of this life. At home, a pross has a man that's stronger than all the fellows she sees day and night. I'm not talking about physical. It's mental. Once you get in a woman's head, you've got her body.

The rules of the life devolve from a strong, dominant mack. You don't let a little girl come to you once with no money and then give you three or four hundred dollars and run off and come back again. That's against the rules. You're not supposed to take another man's woman and don't notify him. But you might go against the rules to enforce them later on. Sometimes you can't depend on the other fellow. He might not be true to the game and understand cop and blow. That's when you cop a girl and lose her. There's also cop and lock, when she don't blow no more. That's also called cop and hold.

I'm a mack and I'm supposed to be down for money. I might take a woman knowing that she didn't give me money, because later on I know she will. I accept her and wait for money.

I had Lisa for four days in Cleveland. Sexually I had her. That's against the rules. She hadn't even chose me. She didn't give me no money. But the rule is really to get her to New York. My objective was to have her follow me anyplace. Lisa had been in the life. I knew if I got her here she would be cool. She said, "I want to choose you."

I said, "I don't want no Cleveland money."

"I want to choose you."

"I don't want nothing from you." I was psyching her. "I just want you to come to New York with me." I knew in New York everything would be all right, because I'm Mr.-Up-and-Coming-Black-East Side. "Just be my woman. Come on and try me." I was using that as a trick. I gave her the impression I cared for her. We went out and swung and talked. A girl can't stand to have you say, "Give me money." You have to make a woman say, "This is who I want to have my money. This man is going to make me good." Most women want a man to be their everything.

A lot of women be whores and don't know it. They be going out with Tom, Dick, or Harry and having Peter, Paul, and Mary—accepting favors or rent money. They be whores. It just takes a pimp to enlighten them to the fact that they've been whoring all along. Of course, some women never know what they were meant to be in life.

Iceberg Slim was an old-time pimp—vulgar. He was cold on his bitches' ass. Now a woman isn't the dumbest individual in the world and if you call her bitch and bitch and bitch, she just can't stand you. Iceberg had a barbaric approach. He kidnaped women and hit them if they didn't come up with their dues— he put the fear of God in them. One morning, he was riding in his automobile—air-conditioned. He'd just picked up a woman from work. He said, "Crack the window." She said, "Why do you want the window cracked, Slim?"

"To let out some of this odor. You stink, bitch. I smelled something stinking. Some of that funky odor. Open the window and let it out. This ain't no house." The girl had been working all night long.

That's pretty strong language. Today we're more elite. I do say, "Baby, I need money and I'm tired. Things ain't coming up to par." You can't be weak. If a woman says she's sick, you can't tuck her in bed and put a thermometer in her mouth. You've got to say, "No. That won't do. You've got to have a hundred. You have to do better." Never say die. It's a pride within yourself.

The old-fashioned pimp walks ten paces behind a girl when she picks up a trick. He sees the trick is tipsy and thinks he can get more out of him. So he follows him up to the hotel room and waits till the guy's pants are at the end of the bed. Once a trick gets a piece of ass, he loses his mind. The pimp goes over his clothing and takes everything he's got on his person. But maybe the trick isn't such a chump and he wakes up and tries to defend himself. The pimp didn't think this would occur. Now somebody's not going to come out of that hotel room. Today that man would not be considered a pimp. He's just a robber with a girl. A pimp does not rob.

Me and Silky would never get involved in that. We simply wouldn't be available. We do not walk down the street hand and hand with our girls. A fellow who does that doesn't keep his girls for long. If he do, there's something wrong with the girls. 'Cause that's not how to ho. Real professionals—they would like their woman in Bangkok while they're in Iran. I like to be as far away from my women as possible—if my women are trustworthy and can take care of their business without me.

Love can ruin a relationship in this life. I've seen people completely destroyed by love. 'Cause she can't stand to see him with other women. And he can't bear the thought of her out trying to get him money with other men. Time may change the way you pimp, but love should never enter the relationship between a pimp and his ladies.

Iceberg Slim forced women to be with him. He was right there at the post with a pistol, keeping watch over her twenty-four hours a day. That's pimping alley style. In this time and era, there's very few fellows that have enough gumption to do that, and if they have the gumption, they wind up in the can for good.

You could force a woman through dope—through injections in her arm. But there's very few kept that way and they've usually been junkies before. If a woman wants to be with you, she's going to be with you. If she ain't, she ain't. Every woman I know that's with a man, love him. If she doesn't, she's fucked up mentally. It's hard enough to hold a woman—let alone get

her to get you money. This is a consensual relationship. You can only have who will have you.

When a woman crosses you, you can use ass-whipping or fire them. Some of them get dropped like a hot potato. Some of them get whopped and smacked around. You can give them a good tongue-thrashing and sometimes just sweet conversation. It depends. But if you have more than one chick, each girl knows there's another one behind her. That's the best discipline you have.

Silky has a chosen personality and way about him. He was a born little mack. A born ladies' man. Like I am. Anywhere he went, he highlighted. He didn't have to play it. Any little girl in town, you'd say, "Do you know Silky?" and she'd say, "Yeh." He had a natural quality about himself to captivate them.

I was always meant to be a pimp. Silky was always meant to be a pimp. He came by my house one day with a little girl. He wanted to fuck her. He took her in my room and balled her. I had two bedrooms and every bed was full of women. I said, "Why do you need this shit? When are you going to sell that motherfucker?" Three months later, he got a girl. He's been selling it ever since and doing a damn good job.

Silky was a baby when he started. Other players used to send him milk when he went to night spots with his ladies. He drunk it. It's like kings growing old and getting ready to get off their throne and seeing their successors. These old guys seen it. I think for the way Silky's mastered his own throne at such an early age, he's uncanny. I feel deep in my heart about it, because I knew him from a kid. He never asked me what to do about Christina, or do you know a lawyer. He just did it.

Now he's very sharp, very tricky, and very elite. I like seeing him this way. He'll never know what it means to me. I was the one who enlightened him. We were both popular as squares. Then we started saying, "Bitch, you can't have me no way unless you give me money."

"What do you mean? Sell it?" she says. I mean blip, blop, de bam, scooby do. That is kicking it. That's what you're going to have to do.

This profession takes a man with sharp mental perceptions about life. He has to have a strong mind. You can't be a bird-brain and handle this. You live the game and you learn it. I try to carry pimping with great respect and esteem. Not everyone can be a pimp. Some men look at you with envy and jealousy, because they failed. I've just got to be the best. I was a blue-blood anyway. Now I'm a thoroughbred.

DANDY & SILKY

Dandy: [Angry] Me and you was trying to get some tickets to that Ali fight and I was in the shower when they come out boxing.

Silky: [Defensive] I tried to get hold of you.

Dandy: But I made my plans around you.

Silky: I didn't have no plans. And your phone was out of order.

Dandy: You could have called the apartment building.

Silky: I didn't know the name.

Dandy: You've had me call *your* apartment building a thousand times.

Silky: All I knew was that your phone wasn't working and my phone wasn't working.

Dandy: You could have sent Huckleberry Finn by the apartment and said, "Look man, I'm going to the fight," and whatever. I didn't go out of the house until one o'clock waiting for you.

Silky: [Adding to his defense] I was right here. Linda called me thirteen times, because I told her if I could get tickets she could go. So that's bullshit. I was supposed to meet someone at eight, but I didn't meet him until nine. I got my tickets then and there, saw the fight, and after . . .

Dandy: [Interrupting and interested] Where'd you sit?

Silky: [Flaunting] Ringside, of course. I just told anybody and everybody I'd double their money if they'd sell me their tickets. Someone came through.

Dandy: [Changing the subject and proud] I've got a new chick.

Silky: A new chick?

Dandy: She found me in a women's clothing store—I'd been buying coats and wigs and outfits for my ladies.

Silky: Everyone went to the fight to show off.
Dandy: I saw one picture that looked terrific. She had on a mink coat and mink hat and mink pants. And he had on a mink hat that broke all the way down and all the way around—white pants, silk shirt, and a coat with mink on the collar. I was really down for that fight. I had a new outfit.
Silky: I just went sporty. I had on my white mink jacket and my white mink cap. A turtleneck, and a red-white-and-blue pair of boots. All-American. Did you see the film of the fight?
Dandy: [Resentful] I seen it. You know where I seen it. On my television set at home on the news, and part on closed circuit at a pub with all the aristocrats. I seen Frazier leading with Clay.
Silky: Frazier never stopped. He never stopped. Clay was kid-
46

ding. He was like a punching bag. I was sitting in the same row with Nancy Wilson.

Dandy: I'm so mad that you even went to that fight that I don't want to know they fought.

Silky: Frazier was the Great White Hope.

Dandy: Ali said next time they're going to have to get a judge from out of the country.

Silky: He said next time the judges would come from the moon.

Dandy: Ali talks about Sputnik all the time.

Silky: Frazier is a family man and his wife wants him to retire.

He might. His trainer suggested he not fight again. He just might not fight.

Dandy: But he could go on entertaining in clubs.

Silky: He could go into any *white* club. Clay says anybody who doesn't think Frazier's white should take another look. The Great White Hope just happened to be black. It was strictly a prejudicial fight. White sentiment was for Frazier. He's an Uncle Tom. When they asked Ali, he said he thought Frazier and he should get ten million apiece for getting into the ring. When they asked Frazier, he said, "I'm getting plenty of money. Yes, marster." That's what he should have said. He said it.

Dandy: Whitey can't get around it. Ali represents the new black man. A lot of blacks are glad Frazier got the title because he's black. But the new black man is represented by Ali, and they're the majority.

Silky: Frazier's an all-American black.

Dandy: But I don't feel like every black cat should be a black nationalist.

Silky: Our people was born struggling. I was born struggling. That's what keeps me going. You too. Even in this life. I ain't going to spend no money no more. I'm just going to stack. I'm going to get ten dollars and let it sit in my back pocket. No more jumpsuits. No more shoes.

Dandy: You're out of your peapicking mind.

Silky: I'm not going to get nothing.

Dandy: Wait till you see the shoes I got today. I didn't have a dime. I said, "Put them in the back and I'll be back. No later than Friday." They were something fly—suede with the wet look on top of suede and heels.

Silky: Too loud.

Dandy: No, perfect.

Silky: I have some red-white-and-blue ones, and even they're too much.

Dandy: Part of the profession demands that you be dressed in 1975 style in 1971. You've got to be at least four years ahead of the styles. If you're not going to dress, you're giving up pimping.

Silky: This is the first year I'm not going to get a winter suit.

Dandy: If it is, it will be the last. You can't wear last year's clothes in New York. Everyone else will run you out of here. You can't go on the stroll in T-shirts. Over on Lexington, you've got to take numbers and sign autographs and take contracts and give orders.

Silky: I'm sincere this time.

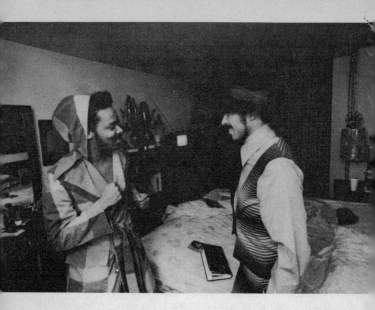

Dandy: There's a hell of a difference between us.

Silky: [Kidding] Generation gap.

Dandy: That ain't the gap. I bridge the gap. I was the fellow taking steps and laying the groundwork for the fellows coming along—like you.

Silky: I went in another direction. I was in another part of the country.

Dandy: There wasn't no part of the country I hadn't been through and laid the groundwork. 'Cause I was from the country. All over the country.

Silky: It wasn't being done in French Lick, Indiana, when I got there. Did you know there was a French Lick, Indiana? I was eighteen and down and dirty then. I had girls out working for four or five hours and their toes was frostbited. I was just a baby.

Dandy: You were responsible for what you did.

Silky: Okay, Uncle Dandy.

Dandy: You've always been a very assertive young kid!

Silky: I'm going to be a *King*. How long did Solomon live?

Dandy: A thousand years.

Silky: How many wives did he have?

Dandy: A thousand.

Silky: That sure's the secret to a long life!

50

PLAYERS

Frankie is deep into nothing, *comments Silky*. He's thinking about nothing. He had eight girls and he was coming. He never branched out into separate apartments for each girl, but he had a Rolls-Royce and clothes and jewelry. Frankie was here in New York a year before I was and he was doing well, as we'd all expected him to do when he decided to make it in the Big Apple. But then he went to the Village. Instead of the Village becoming part of him, he became part of it.

Today's the first time he admitted that he's lost his Rolls. It was put in the city pound when he was arrested on a narcotics charge, and he can't afford to get it out. The car's been in for a year and a half at ten dollars a day. He's been in jail on a narcotics charge, and his girls are gone. No help came.

Now there's been times when I didn't have anybody. But you have to mobilize from there. But Frankie is down and dirty and he can't put it together. His number-one girl, Twiggy, is waiting for him now and I don't think he's going to be able to persuade her back. He's lost a sense of himself as a player.

Dandy: [Answering the phone] You over at my house, Twig? Okay, I'll be there in ten minutes. Frankie isn't saying anything right now. [To Frankie] Hey, here's Twig.

Roger: [To Frankie] Hey, man. Wake up. What'd you say?

Frankie: I said hello.

Dandy: [To phone] He says hello, Twig.

Silky: Let me speak to her when you're through. I'm not dangerous. I just want to say hello.

Dandy: Who's going to get her? Come on, Frankie. If you don't hurry up and get on the job, you're not going to have her and one of us will. You can lie down on the job and just die off and you'll make things more congenial for me. But I just hate to have dead people in my presence, so come alive, man. And take care. I mean, a broad ain't that much.

Roger: You're being made a fool of.

Dandy: I don't understand you, Frankie. As many times as you've bumped your head against the wall in those after-hour joints, and thrown champagne bottles against the wall and let every little girl stole you. I don't understand. It isn't in the game for you to go down the garbage can at twenty-three. I'm forty years old and I ain't thrown none of it away. Yet.

Silky: [Laughing] That's the first time you ever, ever told the truth. You had to be at least forty, 'cause you walked me to elementary school.

Dandy: But I never told you a wrong thing. If I couldn't tell you the right thing, I wouldn't tell you anything at all. Or I'd give you my opinion and let you put it together.

Silky: And I appreciate it man.

Dandy: [To Frankie] Twig's been at my house all evening, and if you want to go and get your broad, man, come on and go with me and get your woman. You going?

Roger: He's going. He's going.

Dandy: I got action and if you're going, go. I'm dead serious. You jam the broad and damn her, or a dude is coming to take her to Boston in a very few minutes. I'm telling you for real. *Me* and her got a friendship going that might turn into a real relationship.

Silky: If you ain't going, Frankie, I'd sure like a chance at her.

52

Dandy: Well, you can take one. [To Frankie] I come to you for her, but if you're not going, I'd just as soon everyone had a crack at her.

Silky: The boy don't feel good. It's that simple.

Dandy: But I'm dead serious. You catch her tonight or she's gone. She's trying to work her way back to you indirectly. But the lady's going to cool and you're going to renege. Now Silky's half-dead and still on his way out the door. We're two charming men with plenty of game and you let yours go to waste. I've been through hell and carnation to get that lady, so you could have her. Now you all got her and you want to let her go. Man, I ain't going to sell me until the last breath is out. I mean, on my death bed, I'll be telling my sons to be real live kings and gentlemen and scholars. True pimps. Now Frankie, let her catch you while you're low down and dirty, and she'll know she's got to get seriously busy.

Roger: [To Frankie] I know how you feel, man. That's why I went to Europe. I got tired of it, man. I just didn't want to see another lady. But I'm back and ready to work, and that's where it is.

Frankie: I'm just down, man.

Dandy: Oh, shit.

Roger: If you don't go after that broad now, man, you're closed up.

Dandy: I appreciate the shot at the lady, but you didn't introduce me to the shot. I made that possible for myself. I've got quite a few things working. I've just got to put them together. But that there lady was already in your plans. That's easy to put together.

Frankie: What plans?

Roger: Twiggy.

Frankie: Oh, I spoke to her today. She's ready. She's a real nice chick.

Roger: If you lose her, you lose part of your strength. She's part of your foundation and if you lose any part of it, you're going to get weaker. If you get her back, you'll gain some strength. I know what I'm talking about.

Frankie: I don't need any more of this bullshit.

Roger: Then go, man.

Dandy: I'm your friend. And I'm a man. Now what kind of friend will call you up and say, "Get over here." I could have her for myself. But I tell you to go, man. If we put our best foot down, one day we'll all go back and buy Cuyahoga County. Here you is letting us down. You young hot wonder, letting the county down.

Roger: This ain't no play, man. This is real. I just don't like to see anyone fall by the wayside.

Silky: I know what you're saying, man. I know him better than anyone in the city, and I just can't reach him.

Roger: He's ready to listen.

Silky: What do you mean, "He's ready to listen"? We brought him here to the girl who made him. . . .

Dandy: [Interrupting] He says she's at my place and gives up.

Silky: I would have took you for your word if you said it was all right.

Dandy: I never said it was all right. I didn't even say she was mine. I said she was his.

Roger: It's hard to come back to a woman just like that. If he was up it would be different.

Dandy: You just don't understand. When a man's down, it makes the ladies more dedicated. And it makes more of a professional of the man. When you're down and out, that's when you're supposed to be at your best. Get me in the corner and up against the wall, and I come out like a cat. Fighting. If she won't have me down, then she can't have me when I'm up. You say, "Come here and have a word with me, woman. It's been a long, long time, baby. But didn't we have fun when and where!"

Roger: [Picking up] "Mama, I need a haircut."

Dandy: "Let's get it together."

Roger: "Mama, I need a new pair of shoes."

Silky: He's at the very, very bottom from almost the top. He's been cute for a whole year by hisself. It ain't cute no more.

Frankie never got his girl, *Silky explains*. He ain't got no girls no more. He's sinking down. He goes to gay bars and throws champagne bottles against the wall.

54

SANDY

The ideal woman for a pimp is my Sandy. When I first met her, *Silky recalls,* she was stripping in Washington, D.C. She asked me questions all the time, and I knew she was interested to a degree. But she'd never had a pimp before. Sandy's conservative now, but she was *real* conservative then. You never would have known she was a stripper. She was quiet and dainty and proper. She seemed so content that I really didn't make a play for her. But I began to go out with her closest friend. Me and Sandy were close, but it wasn't personal.

I'd talk to her about working. We'd sit over drinks and she'd ask me about how a girl got started in the life. I was trying to convince her, not for myself, but for herself. Finally she left the fellow she was with and went to Miami to work. She'd call me in New York and I began to know that she was interested in me personal. Then she came to New York looking for me. I was out of town, but when I came back, I found that she'd been at different clubs I used to go to. I caught her in Washington and took her out. We made an agreement of some sort. She had some business to clean up, and two or three weeks later she came to New York with four thousand dollars for me.

Sandy's been with me for three years. We haven't had four misunderstandings in that time. About once a year, Sandy gets nervous about one of the younger, prettier girls. She worries that I'll forget her. But then we talk about it and that's over till next year.

Sandy is understanding and patient and dedicated. She makes a lot of money and she's mature. She doesn't like her work, but she knows that, to have me, she has to work. To please me is the only thing Sandy cares about. We don't see each other often. But we talk all the time. She'll call and say, "I miss you." I'll say, "I miss you too, baby." These are the sacrifices that a person makes in the life. We're working toward our

goals and our future. During this time, we often can't be together as much as we'd like. I spend more time trying to hold
immature girls who need more attention than Sandy. In that
sense, it may be advantageous to be immature. I see a girl who
acts up and try to quiet her down and keep her. I don't see
Sandy, because I can depend on her. Sandy has a sure and secure position with me. As long as she is the Sandy she is now,
she will have me and she can count on me. If she worked
against that, she'd be like the other girls. Then I would pimp
her—try to get as much out of her as I could. Sandy's not getting
pimped. She's with a pimp. She doesn't just want to be part of
the group that's getting pimped. My and Sandy's relationship is
all preparation for the future.

Sandy has become as dedicated as I am. If I called her and
told her to come over and she had something important to take
care of, she'd take care of that thousand-dollar date. Or one

hundred or two. Any of my other girls would cancel that date and come see me.

I'm really in love with Silky. I wouldn't be here, *says Sandy,* if I wasn't. I believe that he cares for me. I wouldn't go as far as to say he's in love. Silky cares for all his girls. If he doesn't, the girl won't stay. Any woman can tell if a man doesn't feel for her.

It's not an easy life for a pimp. I know one cop well. He's picked me up off the street ever since I've been in New York. He sees Silky driving up in his car, and he'll say, "You can always tell a pimp by his car." Then he'll add, "Boy, I wish I had that life. All those girls out working, while he's riding around in his car and going to bars and having a good time." That cop doesn't realize what a pimp's life is.

Take for instance Silky. He usually has five or six girls, and all these girls call each other up and say, "I did this with Silky," "Silky took me to the Apollo yesterday," "He bought me a coat last week." Then they call him up and say, "How come you bought her that and you didn't buy me anything?"

This goes on constantly. I've been in his house and his phone didn't stop ringing all day. It was girls complaining about this and that—just silly things that the average person wouldn't even think about.

All I can say to the cop is, "Look. You're married. You have a wife. Is it hard for you to keep your wife happy?"

"Yuh, it's kinda hard."

I say, "Well, try to keep five or six of them happy. You'll see how easy it is."

I'm used to living nice and I'm always going to live nice. Now I give Silky all my money. I make about fifteen hundred a week. But he pays for my apartment, my phone bills, my clothes—everything I need. I live in my style and I have Silky.

I don't feel strongly about money because I was poor. I came from money, but I've been too proud to go home and ask my family for it. I've always had to get it for myself. I couldn't make it as a secretary. I tried that. The time clock was not for me. So I started stealing cars. When my father found out, he put me in a Catholic home. I was locked up there for two years.

After I got out of the home, I started forging checks and doing credit cards. My best friend turned me in for forging. She got scared and thought she was going to help me. I'm sure they put innocent people away. Or people who don't belong in jail. I didn't belong there. I was only eighteen and I didn't know nothing from nothing. I was a green kid. But they turned me

57

into a hardened criminal. I got five years, but only did two.

After two years in jail, you don't ever want to go back. It's the most awful experience, but you can benefit even from that. I learned a lot. I read more than I ever did before. I read the entire library three times. I still have a taste for reading. You can learn about people from books—about their lives and their ways of thinking. Why they ended up the way they did. I also used to go to group therapy and listen to people talk. It was the only way to pass time in the penitentiary.

When I got out, I still wanted money and a high style of living, so I started working as a stripper in a club in Washington and turned a few tricks on the side. Prostitution is the only way to make money that doesn't have much time. You can only get ninety days. I never want to go to jail again.

All the girls who work in clubs are hustlers. But those girls are in a particular kind of hustle. They really save their money. All the strippers I know have something to show for it. They have nice homes, small businesses.

I knew one girl who never went out on a date. She made about a thousand a week talking to guys. The hardest thing to learn is the vulnerability of the man. You have to make yourself believe that this man is stupid enough to believe anything you tell him. And he is. One girl called me over to her table and she would say, "This is Sandy. My girl friend. She just got in the business and the wardrobe lady is downstairs waiting for her to pay for her dance outfit. She'll wear the gown just for you this show. Sit right up front and watch her." Meanwhile, I've had the gown for a month. But he'd go right into his pocket and give me the hundred dollars—like it was nothing. It shocked me. He wouldn't go into his pocket and give his wife a hundred dollars. He wouldn't give her ten!

In the meantime, I started turning tricks on the side. In a club, you get offers every single night. I was living with a man— I'd been living with him for four years. He was black, but he sure wasn't a pimp. I never even considered one. I couldn't imagine a girl being foolish enough to give her hard-earned money to some guy who didn't work.

I started falling away from my man, and then I met Silky at a party. He'd just come to town. The minute I saw him, I was attracted, but I said, "I've got to get away from him. He's a pimp and I'm not paying no pimp." I put my best friend in front of me, which is a dirty thing to do. I figured she could handle him. Every time he came over to our apartment, I'd say, "You came to see Jean. Wait a minute. I'll get her." Or I was just leaving. I really tried to stay away from him. I'd talk to him on the phone for hours. I don't even remember what he talked about. We became really good phone friends.

He'd say, "You're just wasting your time."

I said, "So what? I get high every day and make my money."

Then he tried to get me to come up to New York for a weekend. I knew if I came, I'd choose him. I didn't want to. He'd say, "If you can't do it for anyone else, do it for yourself." So I went to Miami and started to work seriously. I wasn't planning to choose him. We'd talked, but I hadn't made up my mind. Then I lost touch.

That's when he got beat up real bad. He gave another pimp's girl some money to go down and get his ladies out of jail. She blew the money, so he kicked her ass. Her fellow went and got a couple of other fellows and beat Silky up. The doctor thought he'd never have any kind of face again. But he was a good doctor and put him back together.

Silky called my old boy friend and left a number for me to reach him. I came back to Washington and he said, "Your friend Silky called and left a number for you. Do you want it?"

Just the way he said it, I said, "No. It's all right."

I went to see my friend Jean one night and answered the phone. It was Silky. He told me what happened and said he was coming down. He was late as usual. I'm not used to having guys late for me, so I didn't pick him up. He said, "I'm coming all the way down to Washington to meet you and you don't even pick me up at the plane." Like he's not used to me either.

We went to one party and then another. Silky kept saying to Jean, "I've just got to have this girl. I've just got to have her."

He stayed down in Washington for three weeks and we were out every single night, partying. But I didn't choose and I didn't go to bed with him. Pimps aren't supposed to sleep with girls unless they choose. Finally he said, "I'm going back to New York and if you want to come with me, you can."

I said, "Silky, you really don't understand. I've been tied up with a guy for four years and this is the first time I've been on my own and I don't want to give it up."

He said, "You can still be your own woman."

Me and my girl friend got in a big argument, because she really dug Silky and I was seeing him so much. She wanted to be with him, but she didn't want to give up her man. We got into a fist fight and I had to pack my stuff and leave.

I went to see Silky and he tricked me. I made a bet with him that I could make more money working the clubs than on the street. I did and then I gave him the money. He said, "That's disgustingly nice." And so I'd chosen.

Silky used to be a real loud, prancing pimp. He wore pink suits and kicked everybody's ass every day. He had all black girls and he had to beat them. Black girls have a lot of larceny.

Before he met me, Silky didn't have any white girls. He wanted to get into white girls. He says they're softer and sweeter than black girls. I've talked about all these things with him. You can get close to a black person, but you always feel a thin line you can't cross. I've been around black people for a long time. I've mostly always had black guys. If I was the only white person in a group, I would forget all about race until somebody new came in. They'd draw attention to it: "You're the only white girl here."

People say that black pimps have white girls so we can pay back for all the slavery they went through; now they got somebody white they can tell what to do. This is true in the case of some pimps. I know pimps who have white girls and hate them. I know one guy who maliciously beats girls, ties them up, and kidnaps them. The girls stay. I've seen girls that started out so pretty and their fellows beat them up so bad they look horrible now. These girls prefer the brutal relationship. You see it all the time.

I could never be with anybody like that. If someone beat me, I'd be gone. I'm old enough and mature enough to sit down and talk if something is wrong. If you can't explain why it's wrong and I can't learn by that, then we don't have a relationship. Silky doesn't like to beat his girls. He's gotten to the point where he doesn't want that kind of girl. Every time he has to do it, he's in a terrible mood. He'd much rather talk it out.

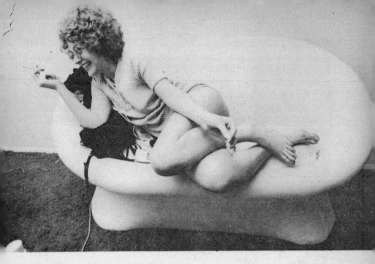

Before I came with Silky, he didn't take questions. If a girl asked him, "Why should I work now?" he'd say, "Don't ask. Just do it." After I chose Silky, he took a lot of time with me, so I could understand. I'd ask him a million questions, because I've got to know.

I asked square girl's questions, because basically I'm a square person. I'd say, "Why would anyone want to give up all their money to you anyway?" "I don't believe a man can care for a girl and let her go out and sell pussy like that." That's the way I felt about it.

He said, "A pimp is a job like a whore is a job. If you were working and I were working and we were square, we'd still put our money together the same way." That is a logical answer.

When I first met Silky, I partied all the time. Silky made me stop. I asked him why. He said you're not supposed to party and go to bars where pimps hang out. You can't even go to the movies without asking. He explained that if someone saw me, it would look like I just ran around, had a good time, and didn't work. That would reflect on Silky and he's very much one for image.

I used to love to dance; at parties, I'd dance all night long. But Silky would never dance with me. I wondered why. Silky said that if a pimp gets up and dances with his woman, it's like you're equal with him. You're not. Silky must keep the pimp-whore thing going.

I'd say, "What's the matter with me talking to a fellow and getting in his car for a run?"

He'd say, "You can't do that. You're not supposed to give any other pimp any kind of play. If you stand around with a pimp, he thinks you're interested. You can't get in a pimp's car. Then he thinks you want to choose."

These are rules we have to follow. Silky takes it for granted that all the girls know them. The rules aren't arbitrary. They're part of a pimp's ego. If a girl runs around, she might see someone who's better than her fellow and say good-bye.

I had never been on the street before I met Silky. He said I had my nose up in the air about the street. He wasn't as broad-minded as he is now. He wasn't aware of the potential of building up a phone business. Everybody had to go out on the street.

I was staying with him at a hotel in Washington and working the clubs. Silky wanted a white girl so bad that he let me slide and didn't force me on the street. I had problems at the clubs, because I'd always spoken badly about pimps to my friends. I said, "These crazy pimps." I used to talk like they were nothing. I used to look down on them—the stereotypes of loud-talking guys who beat their girls. I'd known pimps for a long time because I hung around with people in the life. I didn't have any respect for them.

Pimps used to get mad at me and my girl friend, because we were both stripping and turning tricks and we weren't paying nobody. The pimps called us "the stars."

So all my friends turned against me when I chose Silky. They said, "You're the one who always said you would never have a pimp. You're making a mistake. You're going to be sorry." In Washington, no one had ever heard of a girl who was happy with a pimp.

One night I didn't do so good at the clubs and got disgusted. "The hell with it. I'm going out on the street." Down in Washington, I knew where to go, but I didn't know what to do. So I just went out. I was so proud of myself. I came home and said to Silky, "Guess where I've been? I went out on the street and made a hundred ninety dollars."

I've worked the street off and on ever since. I don't really like the street. From a practical point of view, it's costly. You always have to pay somebody off. You're always getting fines and going to jail and paying lawyers. I'm still terrified of jail. But Silky is the man I want to be with and this is what I have to do to be with him. I don't think I'll ever like being a prostitute.

Silky: [Very serious] Hello, Sandy. Go sit down.
Sandy: [Afraid] Hi.
Silky: [Stern] Ready for a conference?
Sandy: What's the matter?
Silky: I want a joint first. Roll me one.
Sandy: You want a joint . . .
Silky: Three of them.
[Sandy moves to the bedroom to prepare the joints and, when she opens the door, discovers her present.]
Sandy: Silky . . . [gasps] Isn't he adorable . . . oh, Silky. You shouldn't have done it.
Silky: [Pleased with himself] Come on and laugh.
Sandy: I love him.

Silky: Repeat that for me.

Sandy: Where's he going? [To dog] Hi, sweetie pie. [To Silky] What do you call him?

Silky: [Teasing] Whitey. You like that name?

Sandy: No.

Silky: What did you think when I called and told you I was mad and to come by here when you finished working?

Sandy: I didn't know. I was thinking and I couldn't think of anything I'd done bad. How long did you have him?

Silky: I got him this afternoon.

Sandy: [Laughing] I should call him J.W.—Just Whoring. (Note: Silky's dog is J.P.)

Silky: It's not a girl. Did you think you'd been a bad girl or something?

Sandy: I knew I hadn't. But I said, "Don't blame yourself, Sandy." And look how pretty he is. [Pulls a present from her purse] I got you a wallet from Scandinavia.

Silky: Is this the way it opens?

Sandy: Careful. There's some money m there.

Silky: Let's start with the hundreds.

Sandy: I don't know why, but this looks like a woman's wallet.

Silky: Yeah. I don't like it.

Sandy: [Apologetic] I'll change it. I'll get you another.

Silky: I can stand anything with green in it. I'll trade you when you get another one. Remember. Last time you gave me a wal-

let, you got excited in court about my traffic ticket and you left
the wallet on the seat in the courthouse. How much was in it?
Sandy: [Sheepish] Five hundred.
Silky: I bet you was laughing at me instead of the judge.
Sandy: I wasn't hardly laughing.
Silky: I'll never get over it.
Sandy: And I brought you some new massage cream . . . I've
got to go. [She picks up the dog.]
Silky: You can get the dog tomorrow morning.
Sandy: I want to take him now.
Silky: You going back home now?
Sandy: [Sadly] I got a date.
Silky: See you in the morning.

A woman's relationship with a pimp must be selfless. Most women are very self-centered. They like all the attention. It's hard to care more about someone than yourself. It's hard to try to understand another person. I'm very old-fashioned. It gives me great pleasure to give myself completely to my man.

For a long time, I knew Silky, but he didn't know me. I've never met a guy like Silky. With some fellows, it's a sex thing. That's their game. But with Silky, it really isn't. It's more an understanding—a talk game that isn't a game.

Silky has a very heavy head. You can discuss anything with him and he has the answers. If he doesn't, he'll never let you know.

In the last eight months, Silky's gotten to know how I think. I sit around my apartment reading and thinking all the time. I acquired a taste for quiet times in the penitentiary. Sometimes I get to the point where I think so much I wonder if I'm crazy. Like Silky will tell me he's going to keep Linda at his apartment for a while. I'll start thinking. I figure out why he's doing this. I can't keep it to myself. So I run it down to Silky: "Are you keeping Linda at your house, because you're afraid, if you leave her on her own, she'll blow? Like she's so dependent now she couldn't stand to stay alone?"

Silky starts laughing. He says, "That's just why I'm doing it." He's so innocent—the way he lets it all hang out. Only he isn't innocent at all.

Silky never talks about me and I never talk about seeing him. That's personal between us. People don't hear about me or see me out with him. They know I've been with him for three years and can't understand. They think he doesn't like me. Different girls call him up and say, "You really don't like Sandy, do you?" He just laughs. It's gotten to the point where I'm a mystery to everyone. Then they decide that Silky really cares about me and that's why he keeps me locked up and never lets me out. He's afraid I'll find another guy.

The truth is I prefer to stay at home. Silky comes about once a week. When I first chose him, I saw him every day, but now I only want to see him once a week. I'd rather be with him for one full day and a whole night than have him come over for an hour and pick up his money and leave. I'm quite content to stay at home.

For the other girls, they're younger, I'm twenty-seven and settled in my ways. They're in their early twenties and consider only today. If Silky doesn't see them for one day, they're ready to leave him.

Part of their problem is that they can't organize time. Take Kitty. She goes out on the street, works and comes home. What does she do? She doesn't even have a TV. You can only sleep so much. That's the beginning of problems. If you have time to lie around thinking about things, you get in trouble. But if I find myself thinking bad things, I just do something to occupy myself.

Silky and I used to predict what his girls would do. Then we gave up. A couple of girls he's had we thought were going to stay and didn't. Like Georgia. She left and then came back. She told me she'd thought all about it and decided she wanted to be with Silky. She was going to be right by him. She was so together. Three weeks later, she ran off. You never know what the girls are thinking about.

Silky's other girls are my wives-in-law. They refer to me as "Mother." I've been with Silky the longest, and they discuss their problems with me when Silky's busy. I try to help them understand him. I want to help him by making the girls stick. You might think I'd be jealous—me being in love with Silky and him having other women. I'm not. I accept the fact that he's a pimp. That automatically means he has other women. Sometimes it's hard when Silky cops a new girl. I'm proud of him, because he's pimping well, but I'm also always a little bit afraid that she'll be nicer or prettier or younger than me and Silky will like her best. But I know that all men are promiscuous. If I were involved with a straight guy, he'd be playing around with other women behind my back. Our relationship would not be honest. With a pimp, you know who he's with and where and when and why. That's why you can have a beautiful and complete understanding.

I have many responsibilities, because Silky trusts me. The car is in my name and I pay the bank notes. If a girl goes to jail or gets a case, I have to go down to court and get her out. Other girls help if I'm busy or out of town, but ultimately, I'm responsible.

I'm trying to get Silky organized. He's always lived for today, but he's beginning to think about tomorrow. Last year, he ran through over three hundred thousand dollars. I can't say where it went. It's not his style to think about saving and investing in businesses. I told him if he'd just save two hundred a week—which is nothing—he'd be surprised at the money he'd have at the end of the year. If I have a suggestion to make, I make it so he feels he's made it. Then I say it's his suggestion and a good idea. He likes to make the decisions.

He doesn't want to make any decisions about my business—dates and tricks. He expects about two hundred dollars a day and that's all he wants to see or hear. The more elevated the pimp, the less he knows about the girls' day-to-day affairs. You learn to take care of yourself. You develop a pride. You can't possibly live in a situation like this unless you are independent.

I work off my phone, in bars, and on the street. Most of my tricks are Mafia. These men pay the best money. They have the most money, but gangsters can't stand pimps. All they ever talk about is how they hate pimps. The other day, a pimp got killed on 48th Street. It had all the marks of the Mafia. They cut his cock off and stuck it in his mouth. That's definietly a Mafia thing.

These gansters come up to my apartment and when their time is up, I tell them to leave. I don't like people sleeping over. They say, "You got a pimp. That's why you want us to go."

I says, "Well, if I had ten black, filthy niggers coming up here after you, it's none of your fucking business." They like you to talk that way. If I sit here all night and deny that I have a pimp, they're not going to believe me anyway. So why bother.

Gangsters aren't the only people who hate pimps. A pimp has the cops against him and most people outside the life. A pimp is a very lonely person. Even with his girls, he can't let his feelings show. Supposing a pimp fell in love with one of his girls. She'd never know, because he's professional. She'd get spoiled and everyone else would leave if he let it out. My relationship with Silky may be special. That's because I've been with him longest. We have a beautiful understanding, but I wouldn't go as far as to say it was love on his part.

We've been through a lot together—more than any of the other girls. More than they'll ever go through, because he'll never be doing as bad as he's done before.

It was horrible when I was his only girl. Before I came with him, I was a terrible romantic. I had to live with a guy. If I had to live by myself, I couldn't stand it. Silky's got me to the point where I prefer to live alone. He's used to having a lot of money and at least three women. When everyone else left, I was by myself with him. It was bad. He didn't have a car. He was looking for girls, but it's hard with no car and no money to get around on. So Silky just stayed in his apartment, never went out, and got skinny. I used to go and stay with a girl friend and come home to him every three days or so. People would say, "Now that you have him to yourself, why don't you stay with Silky all the time?"

I'd say," 'Cause I can't stand to live with him." I do want to have his children, but I'd live with the children and he'd visit. Silky's good with kids, but, of all the pimps we know who have kids, their woman takes advantage. Silky has to feel that I won't stop working because I have his child. He hasn't gotten to that point yet. I think he's also got to get out of himself more. If he feels like it, Silky will clam up and shut you out.

Silky can get in very bad moods. Specially after he's spent lots of money. One day he paid for all my court cases. That was a nice piece of money. Then he paid the car-repair bill. Then he paid Linda's bail. I could see he was in a bad mood. I tried to make him laugh and he wouldn't. Usually I can break him out of a mood. The phone kept ringing. He must have gotten up twenty times for the phone. I finally said, "I'm going home."

If you're with a fellow for a long time and stay in his corner, he depends on you, and you're going to be as lonely as he is. He takes you for granted. If he needs something, he can call you and know it will be taken care of. You never see him. Everyone else acts up and gets to see Silky. But you're going to be lonely.

My lonely periods are from six in the morning till noon. If

I've been blowing coke and can't go to sleep, then I get lonely. I don't like to bother Silky, because he's got so many things on his mind. He hardly ever has any time to himself. I feel better if he calls and says, "What are you doing? Come on down." I'd feel ridiculous calling him and asking to come down.

If I find myself thinking the wrong way, I'll call up a girl friend and go over to her house. I would never go out with another man. There's no one else for me. Silky never worries. We talk a lot. Some girls aren't intelligent enough to understand. You have to program them: "Go do this and come home." I'm reasonably intelligent and you can't just tell me to jump out the window. Everything has to have a reason. Silky's spent a lot of time answering, "Why?" Now he doesn't have to tell me. If I have a problem, I think it out. His way.

WINTER

CHRISTMAS

This is the first Christmas I've ever given the girls mink coats, *Silky explains*. They're off work after twelve on the 24th and all day the 25th. It's back to the drawing boards on the 26th.

Silky: You're going to look like Annie Oakley with that hat.
Sandy: I may never take this off!
Linda: This is just lovely. Open one of your presents, Silky.
[Silky removes a diamond cocaine spoon from its box.]
Silky: Think I won't use it or something? Now dig the flip on the flip side. There's diamonds on both sides!

Silky: You're so nervous you don't know what's going to happen. But I promised you a rabbit.

Kitty: I know it's not rabbit fur.

Silky: All of them are mink except yours. What do you know about rabbit fur? Now everybody's waiting on you. Unwrap it. It's only rabbit.

Kitty: [Tired of being teased and fearful] Oh, come on.

Sandy: We're waiting for you.

Kitty: I haven't slept all day waiting to open my present.

Silky: Wait a minute before you open it. Are you going to be mad if it's rabbit?

Kitty: Silky! I know you didn't give me a rabbit coat.

Silky: [Continuing to kid] Isn't rabbit expensive? It's an expensive rabbit coat. What's the matter with rabbit? I say it's a good present.

Kitty: Oh, come on Silky. Cut it out.

Silky: See. It's white rabbit.

Kitty: [Vastly relieved] No. It's not. It's mink. Oh, Silky. [She bursts into tears]

Silky's Aunt: Oh, Silky. That *is* beautiful. [To Kitty, now in his arms] How do you like it?

Sandy: Isn't it pretty? Kitty, you almost had me crying.

Kitty: He almost had me fooled.

Aunt: Well, I'll just take it home. Kitty's crying so much she don't need it.

Sandy: Kitty, you've cried enough tonight.

Aunt: You gonna stop crying?

Kitty: This is white. It's beautiful.

Aunt: Did you style it for Christmas, Silky?

Silky: I picked it out.

You Silky's little girl [to Kitty's baby]? I like 'em big, but I like 'em small too. I mean, I think I've got one vacancy . . .

I saw my mink coat before Christmas, *Kitty explains.* I really don't like mink coats, but this one was sporty and sharp. It's me, and I really wanted it, so Silky bought it. He had Linda come over and wrap all the coats in boxes.

I went to the jeweler's to get his present and when I come back he says, "Guess what?"

"What?"

"I got a surprise for you. I traded your coat." So I figured maybe it was a maxi or a mini. Something better. He said, "It's bad. It's bad. It's a rabbit coat."

I says, "Can I see it?"

"No, it's in a box and it's wrapped up."

"It's rabbit, Silky?" My heart fell.

"Well, I didn't think you liked the other one."

"If you didn't think I liked mink, what makes you think I'm going to like rabbit?"

"But it's bad, Kitty. Let me tell you about it. It's maxi and white rabbit with black spots on it."

I figured I wasn't going to fall for that and started laughing. I said, "You wouldn't do that to me. You wouldn't give me a rabbit and everyone else mink." Then I started crying. I stopped crying. I asked Sandy, who was at his apartment.

Sandy said, "I saw it and it's really bad." I asked her to describe it and she said, "White maxi with black spots."

Then I called up Linda and said, "Silky doesn't know which box my coat is in. There's a red, gold, and green box. He doesn't know which is which or whose is whose."

She said, "Sandy's is in the green one, mine in the gold, and yours in red."

"What's in mine?"

"It's rabbit. That's yours, isn't it?"

I just said, "Thank you, Linda."

Then I started crying and wouldn't even talk to Silky. I went home and started crying again. I was sitting at my house with another girl and we're wrapping Silky's presents and she said, "I don't believe Silky did that, but I'll call and try to make him tell me."

She calls and says, "Kitty is really upset. I won't tell her you're just joking."

He says, "I ain't joking. I got the bitch a rabbit coat and if she don't like it, she don't get nothing."

I call him back and say, "Silky, I'm sorry for acting crazy and I'll take the coat. I want it."

I went over to his place and opened up my goddamned red box and it wasn't rabbit. I just opened it at the corner and started crying. I know he does this to please and tease me. I know he does it to make me happy. I asked him, "How come you did that to me, Silky? People who knew what happened thought I was stupid and people who didn't know thought I was some kind of nut."

He said, "I wanted to surprise somebody. Everyone else knew what they were getting."

Silky could make anyone believe him, but if he told Sandy that he traded her coat for rabbit, she would have said, "Oh, really. If that's what you want me to have, Silky, that's what I want." When she opened up the coat, even if she hated it, she'd say, "It's beautiful." 'Cause Silky wanted her to have it. If he traded her mink coat for rabbit, no matter how much she wanted mink, she would have preferred rabbit. She wouldn't let him know he blew it, because, if she was unhappy, he would be unhappy too. I'm not that cool with him.

KITTY

I've known Kitty for two years, *Silky says*. The improvement in her is night and day. She used to be quite wild. She used to be a troublemaker. She'd crack with all the girls. "Silky this and Silky that." It doesn't take very much for them to upset each other. It might happen that they say something and I never see the girl again. No matter how perfect our relationship may be, it's a delicate situation. My women are professional at offending one another without saying a thing.

Kitty's quit talking. She'll sit down and discuss everything with me. Her feelings toward me have changed. She feels more strongly and she behaves. This is the first time she's ever been emotionally involved with a man. Other fellows get girls and take advantage of them for the time they have them. I try to make my girls mature. I try to help them grow. Kitty is becoming mature.

I'm madly in love with Silky, *Kitty explains*. I don't know which is worse—spending the rest of my life with him or without him. If I left him, I'd be miserable all the time. If I'm with him, I'm miserable some of the time.

There's just something about Silky. He understands all women. Straight guys don't understand. I was going with a straight guy when I was working, and he thought I was cheating on him. So he'd be going out with girls. I asked, "Why are you going out with these girls? I don't fool around. When I want to be with you, I can't because you're busy."

He said, "You be fucking guys all night long. Why can't I fuck girls?" But it's work. It is not for *my* satisfaction. Now, whatever I do, Silky understands. I can come in upset and Silky will automatically know I had a bad night. I'm not turning tricks for the enjoyment of it. I'm doing it for Silky. For the love of him. That makes him appreciate me more.

Sometimes I go over to Silky's and say, "You know, I must have fucked a hundred guys. What do you think about that?"

He says, "How much did they spend?" Shit like that he says.

I says, "Do you think any less of me? I mean, when you call and I say I'm busy and you know I'm having sex with a guy and you say, 'As soon as you're finished, come over here,' and when I come over to you I've just had sex with another guy?"

He says, "You know I like you. I try not to think about you and other guys. When I do, I'm a little sad. But you're lucky to have heart enough to turn tricks or you couldn't have me."

Silky puts all his time into being a ladies' man. Another guy has to go to work. Silky dedicates all his energies to pleasing us. Whatever he does, it's for us. Him and us together. If I was really unhappy, he'd try and get me happy.

Sex is the major part of our relationship. I'm very broadminded about sex. Silky tries to act straight, but he's not. I don't mean he likes guys, but like: "You suck my dick, but I don't suck your pussy." "I'll put it in you, but that's all I'm going to do." Silky used to be very old-fashioned about sex, but I've gotten him to do just about anything. I've turned him out sexually. We have the best sex.

Linda is prudish. Sandy does what Silky does. She makes him the domineering one. I don't become domineering, but I suggest things to him. The only thing Silky won't do is go down on you. That's because he's a pimp. Eventually I can make him do it, if I get him high. I'm always talking about it. It's not fair. Silky will make me suck his dick for three hours. He's an egomaniac and likes making you his servant.

I would like Silky to rape me. Just to pretend. When I asked him, he said, "How the hell can you rape a bitch whose legs are always open?"

You can always tell when Silky is going to have sex with you. If he opens the door and says, "Hi," then you know you're not going to have sex. If he makes a remark like, "I smelled you coming, bitch," you know he will. Then you go to the bedroom and watch TV and talk to him. He'll tell you to rub his back. If he tells you to rub his thighs, that's when he's going to do it. He says, "Massage a pimp's thighs," or "Massage my pretty thighs," "Take off your hat and coat and get in bed with a pimp." He does it the same way every time with all his girls. It's maddening. There's no variety. I always know when I'm going to get it and when I'm not.

One time he forced me to have sex. I didn't want to because I was mad at him. We were lying in bed and he holds out his arm and I put my head on it and pretend to go to sleep. He takes my hand and puts it on his dick. I looked at him, "Silky?"

He says, "What?"

"I don't want to have sex with you." Instead of asking why, he punches me. I don't know how he found me in the dark. I was jumping all over the bed, for real. He just beat the hell out of me.

Then he said, "What did you say?"

"Nothing."

"I don't like the way you said that."

"Nothing."

I was crying and he says, "Put this big black motherfucker in your mouth and maybe that will stop some of the noise." I couldn't even breathe. I was choking. Then he just did it. Afterwards I started laughing. He said, "What's so goddamned funny?"

"That was about the best time we ever had."

He started laughing and said, "I knew you were a freak."

"Yes, and so are you, because you did it." I like to be dominated. That stimulates me—to feel a man is over me and in control.

You find that all pimps have been in bad-boys' school and all whores have been in bad-girls' school. We ask, "What penitentiary were you in?" like, "Where'd you go to school?"

I used to do bad things like stealing cars. They caught me and I went to the penitentiary. I got out and came to New York. I was sixteen and needed a job. I walked into Mickey Walker's on 49th and 8th. I looked out of place. This bouncer came up to me and says, "Can I help you?"

I says, "I had an appointment for a job here. I was supposed to speak to the manager."

I sat down in a booth and this girl came over and told me a friend of hers was at the bar and would like to have a drink with me. I thought this was a good play, because then the manager would think I could get along with people. I went to the bar. I don't drink, but I ordered Chivas Regal, because I knew it was expensive.

I'm just sitting at the bar and the manager comes and gives me the job. He says, "Don't tell me how old you are. You're over eighteen, right?"

"Right."

"That's all I want to know. Don't tell me nothing else."

I'm supposed to be back for work that night. The girl still wants to talk. She asked whether I'd ever partied before. Partying to me isn't two girls and a guy—partying is going out dancing. I said, "Yeah. What do you think I am, a square?" Now a square to me meant a person who doesn't swing.

She looked like she thought I was square. But I'm going to prove I'm not. I'm going to prove myself in the big city. She asks me, "Do you ever go to bed with a man for money?"

I said, "What do you think I am? A prostitute?"

"Do you want to have a party with me and my friend?"

I said, "Yeh." I wanted to meet some people in New York. So we get into this guy's car and go to his apartment in Queens. Today I wouldn't go all the way to Queens with a trick. Unless I knew him and he had a high price.

We go to this guy's house and he asks if I want a drink. I didn't want him to think I was stupid so I said, "Yeh." I was sitting there sipping my drink and there was no people coming. I says, "Where's all the people?"

86

She takes off her clothes and he takes off his and tells me to undress. I don't know where I'm at. I know we drove a long way. Here's a man and a girl and I think they're friends and they want to rape me. So I says to myself, I'm not a virgin. I may as well let them fuck me, instead of having them fight me and beat me up, or kill me and hurt me.

The guy wants to see the girl go down on me. He wants me to go down on her too, but I says, "No. Please don't make me." They didn't, but she really went down on me. Later I learned you're not supposed to with a trick. You just pretend—get down close and fake.

The girl left and I saw the man give her money. Even then I had a bit of game and sense. While he was driving me back, I started crying. He asks me why I'm crying. I said he'd given her money, but he didn't give none to me. By then I knew she was a prostitute. He told me I was an innocent kid and he felt kind of bad. He'd thought I was a working girl. So he gave me twenty dollars. And I started crying again. He said, "Why are you still crying?"

"Because I need forty dollars for my rent. I just came to New York and if I don't pay my rent, I don't have no place to go." So he gave me forty dollars. And then he gave me ten more.

He said, "Now you have a little money. Try not to do this no more." He was really nice.

I goes to my friend's house and I show her the money. "Look I says, I got fifty dollars."

She says, "How did you get this money?" She'd told me the bar was a bad place to go, but I guess she thought I was too innocent to tell me there were pimps and prostitutes and tricks in that bar.

"I got the job and my boss advanced the pay."

"They don't do things like that. I know how you got the money." She tore it up. She told me if I ever needed money to ask her and never to do what I did again. I said okay.

I started working the bar. I got to know prostitutes and pimps. I didn't know they were pimps. They wore lime and lemon and raspberry suits. I thought they were movie stars.

One girl, Candy, kept coming to the bar and bothering me to visit her. I was lonely and finally told her I'd come. I went to her apartment and buzzed. This guy answers. "Candy's not home, but she's expecting you, so come up."

I went up and he started talking to me. "I'm Candy's boy friend and her business manager." I didn't know this added up to pimp. Candy doesn't come home and she doesn't come home. I'm drinking wine and getting high by contact with the reefers coming at me. At last Candy phones and the guy tells me, "Candy's not coming. She went to jail." Really she didn't come just so he could cop me. "She told me you should wait for her."

I was so tired I didn't want to leave. Everything seemed so nice. There was another bedroom and he told me I could stay there.

A couple of hours later he walked in and woke me, "Will you do me a favor? There's this guy here. He wants to see you and he'll give you fifty dollars." He said he didn't want to have sex or nothing. I just had to tell him dirty stories.

Well, this kept happening. These guys kept coming up. He'd come in and say, "Candy's not home, so you have to see this guy." Finally I had sex with one of them. By that time I had three hundred dollars.

Candy came home and said how much she appreciates me seeing all these guys. I says, "Guess what? I made three hundred dollars. I've never had three hundred dollars in my life. I've never seen it in one pile."

She says, "Maybe you should give some of it to him. Just go talk to him. He could hold your money for you."

I went into the bedroom with him and said, "You know, I made three hundred dollars." And I gave him twenty dollars. He didn't do nothing. I did it. He couldn't have made it if I wasn't there.

Then I told Candy I gave him some money.

"How much did you give him?"

"Twenty dollars."

"And you made three hundred? Every day you can make this money. You should make him your manager and your boy friend too."

So I gave him the three hundred dollars, which was all his to begin with, because he'd give fifty bucks to a guy and say, "I want you to give it to the bitch. She'll give it back to *me!*"

Once they knew I would turn tricks, I started taking dates off the phone—twenty-, thirty-, forty-dollar tricks. And then they put me out on the street.

I used to work with one of Silky's girls, Snow, on the street. I didn't know Silky personally, but I thought he was real cute. He was sure of himself and conceited, but that made me really like him, because he had confidence.

I'd talk to him on the telephone. He'd say, "Stacking up my money?"

I'd say, "What do you mean, stacking up *your* money? I'm not even with you."

One night Silky was riding down Lexington Avenue in the El-dorado. He calls to Snow and tells me to come. I'm not going to because, when you get in a pimp's car, you have intentions of being with him. But we gets in the car and goes to a place called the Blue Point and then to his apartment on 48th Street. The apartment was a mess, because his girl, Diane, had just run off. Silky sits down on the couch and says, "All right. Start clean-ing."

I thought, "Who the fuck does this nigger think he is?" I was mad. But I was scared, too. Here I am riding around in a man's car and going to one of his apartments.

He says, "Take all those clothes and put them in the inciner-ator." So I go out to the incinerator and then start in cleaning and cleaning. Snow and I cleaned up the whole apartment.

When we were in the hall dumping garbage, I said, "I'm going to sneak off. Who does this guy think he is?"

She said, "Shut up. How do you think I feel? We're cleaning because, if you choose Silky, this is where you're going to live."

Finally we gets through cleaning and go downstairs to his car. He says, "Oh, I forgot. I've got a surprise for you." And he drives back to the apartment and says, "You all forgot the kitchen. Get back in there and clean up." We finish and he says, "You got expense money?"

Snow says yeah and I say yeah. I didn't know who he was talking to. I was scared. I knew I would have to say yes or no. I knew I would have to tell him whether I'd be with him. Silky says, "Go in the hall." So me and Snow go toward the hall and he says, "Not you. You stay here."

He says to me, "Well, what are you going to do?"

And I says, "I don't know."

"What do you mean by that? Are you going to be my woman?"

"I don't know. You know, I have a baby."

"I know."

"You know my first responsibility is to my child."

"I know that."

"You know I have to take care of the baby. I have to pay the sitter every week."

He said, "We can afford it, can't we?" I kept trying to ignore the question, because he kept saying, "We can afford it, can't we?"

I said, "Yeah."

"You going to be my woman?"

"Yeah." We didn't have no conversation about nothing. I was the easiest girl Silky ever copped. He just jumps into bed

and tells me to massage his pimp's thighs. I went to work that night, and I've been with Silky, off and on, for four years.

I put myself down as a woman. I used to have confidence in myself. Guys liked *me*. Now the only thing I have is sex. I want to be fun to be with. "Wouldn't you like to walk down the street with me?" The only thing between me and Silky is sex. Linda he likes to take out. Sandy he talks to. When he's in a really groovy mood, he'll call me and we have sex.

Anything he wants to do, I do. I have anal sex with him. When we did that, he said, "You're not going to believe this, but I've never done that before."

I said, "Do you think I have?" About two months later, he did it again. Silky has a terrible memory. He knows he's done something, but he can't remember which of us he did it with.

He says, "This is the second time I've done that."

"When was the first time?"

"A couple of months ago."

"Well, why didn't you do it with me first?"

"You should be glad I do it with you at all."

"Well, this is the second time I did it," I says.

"Who'd you do it with before?"

"You don't know?"

"Who?"

"Silky!"

He's always trying to show off when other people are around. I'll be sitting on the couch while he's goofing off with some guys, and if my glance just happens to go to his pants for a minute, he'll say, "Go on and take them down. Don't be shy because Roger's here."

I'll say, "Oh, Silky."

One time after he took a shower, I was drying him. I was on my knees—face to face with his cock. He's always saying, "Go on and bite on the big fellow." I thought I'd call his bluff, because I don't care. Roger was standing in the bedroom door, but I had all my clothes on. So Silky says, "Go on and bite on the big fellow." I just grabbed it and put it in my mouth.

He said, "Bitch. What's wrong with you. Roger's standing there." He pushed me away.

I said, "I'm just doing what you wanted me to do."

"Man, get out of there, Roger." Then he says to me, "How come you got so much heart all of a sudden? You won't suck it in the movies."

"What do you mean, Silky? What was the name of the movie?"

He tries to think. Then he says, "It was Linda." That's really upsetting. He's not sure what he's doing.

Silky is important to me, because I have to prove I can have a healthy sexual relationship. It's particularly important for a prostitute—after you've been with the animals. I never come with tricks, but one time I wondered if I could. I said to myself, "Let's see if this motherfucker can make me come." I closed my eyes and pretended it was Silky. I came. I just tried it one time to see if it worked. I wouldn't again, because that's cheating on Silky.

Mine and Silky's relationship—that's the only thing we have: sex. I'm satisfied with Silky. I'm fulfilled. But I have never come with Silky. I want to, but I get carried away with acting. In most relationships, she's trying to please him and he's trying to please her. In ours, I'm trying to please Silky and Silky's trying to please Silky. Kitty gets left out. That worries me. Sometimes I think I should go to a psychiatrist.

I want Silky to want me for things besides sex. For Silky, I'm a good lay and a good cook. I bring in money, but everyone else does that. Silky don't ever take me out.

One time he got back from traveling and I wanted a night off with him. He really beat me. After he was through, he told me to do a good make-up job, put on a wig, cover up my eyes, and get to work. I've gone out to work with two black eyes.

Silky thinks I turn myself in to the cops to get out of working.

That's silly. If I don't want to work, I can just go home and not answer the phone until five o'clock the next afternoon. I leave a message on Sandy's answering service that I'm staying downtown and I'll be home in the morning. That means I got a *dis con*. If I say, bring money, that means I got a case.

Anyway, I want to work for Silky. I do anything Silky wants, because, when he's happy, he makes everyone else happy automatically.

I massage Silky, because he loves to get massaged. At least twice a day he gets lotioned down. We use baby lotion, because oil makes him greasy. Lotion makes his skin silky.

Just once recently, I had a massage myself. It was fantastic. I felt so alive. I didn't tell Silky, 'cause I thought he might get mad that I paid for it. When he came over to my house on Sunday, I suggested that we get this masseuse over. I told him, "Silky, there's this fantastic lady for massages."

He says, "Is she cute?"

"No."

"Is she old?"

"Yes."

"How old?"

"About fifty."

"Is she white?"

I says, "No."

"Forget it. I only like cutie pies massaging me. When you're massaged, you like to open up your eyes and see a cutie pie there. It makes you feel better. If I open up my eyes and see this old black bitch standing over me, it will take something out of it."

Finally, I convinced him it was so great. He says, "How much does it cost?"

"Ten dollars. If we get her with a table, fifteen."

"You make me sound like a trick. If you go for ten, this is what you get. If you go for fifteen, you can get a little more."

I said, "Silky, don't be silly."

"For fifteen dollars, I can get a little girl and get my dick sucked and everything. I could get two Jap girls for an extra massage."

I just looked at him and said, "Would you?" I really wonder if Silky would ever pay a girl for anything. He's so used to being paid.

I like to try to find other girls for Silky. We're all supposed to. If I bring one of my girl friends over, it's a night off for me, I get to see Silky and I get a little credit for trying to do right. I'm not jealous when he's trying to cop, 'cause I only bring girls that won't go with him. I never leave Silky alone with my friends. If I think he's going to send me away, I fall asleep on the couch.

Silky told me I could go to Connecticut with him for a weekend if I could get a girl to choose. I brought him a girl and I was going to let her choose. She'd just had an abortion, so I knew she couldn't fuck and she said she wouldn't suck. I was getting ready to leave them when Silky said, "Goddamn. It's the first time you've ever offered to leave."

I said, "I ain't worried." He started laughing and I goes home.

Afterwards, she and I were sitting around talking. Silky had told me she was a silly little bitch and she wouldn't choose. She starts talking about Silky—she had a nice time with him and he's really good in bed.

I said, "Yes. That's one of his better qualities."

She said, "Of course you knew."

"Of course." I just wanted to hear her story. She described him. Nobody does it like Silky. Fifteen different positions. It's what I call the "copping fuck." The first one he gives you. He keeps moving around. You're on top of him and he stands up and holds you. He does it to say: "Look what I can do. And that was nothing. Stick around and it will get better." He tries to impress people. (It does get better, but it gets fewer and fewer in between. I'd like it once a day.)

I call him up and say, "Hello, Don Juan."

He says, "Hi."

"You didn't have to fuck her twice."

"Bitch, I don't feel like you fucking with me. I'll call you later." He hung up.

When I saw him, I said, "Listen, Silky. You didn't have to do it twice."

"It's your fault. You left."

I says, "It ain't my fault. I didn't tell you to put your dick in."

He says, "I was just laying on the bed and she starts sucking my dick."

I says, "Sure, Silky. Sure." The girl really did think she was supposed to have sex with him. She doesn't know pimps. But why he was lying on the bed with no clothes on, I don't know.

Silky has mastered the art of pimping. He knows all the angles. He knows how to make a girl say, "I want to be with you." He knows how to make a girl go out on the street, sell her body and give him money. He knows how to make a girl stay with him. He knows how to run her off when he's sick of her. It comes naturally. He doesn't have to try to pimp. He's just the best pimp in town.

Once Silky's car was stolen and I tried to get it back. There was a girl named Bunny Brown. She went back and forth between Silky and another pimp, Flash. Bunny was going to leave Silky and she wanted her diamond ring back. Flash says he gave her the ring and Silky says he did, so Silky wouldn't give it back.

Now when you ride in the car with Silky, he'll often jump out and go into a store and leave the motor running. Bunny was in the car when Silky jumped out this time. She took the car and drove it over to Flash. Flash told Silky he wasn't giving back the car until Bunny got her jewelry.

It looked like I should be mad at Silky, 'cause he'd just left me in jail. I told him I'd get his car back. I started hanging around one of Flash's girls. I looked in every garage of every building where Flash had a girl. The car wasn't in none of them. I figured I might be able to find out from his girl, so I stayed over at her house.

One afternoon, we were in bed playing cards and I didn't have no clothes on. Flash comes in the door and I get under the sheet. Now Flash to me is really sexy. So he pulls off the sheet and says, "What are you hiding down there?"

I went to the living room and put my clothes on. His girl supposedly goes to sleep. Flash comes into the living room and has sex with me. He keeps doing it. He's a fuck freak. I forgot all about finding Silky's car, 'cause Flash kept screwing me. (Note: Three weeks later, Silky returned the pawn ticket for Bunny's ring and Flash returned the car.)

Flash is good to his girls. He has to be. That's all he has going for him. Flash lets his girls go shopping every day, but he can only do material things for his girls. I can get material things for myself. As far as a man-woman relationship, Flash has nothing. He's too old. After he's copped a girl, he comes to her apartment and he's dead tired. Can't do nothing.

Silky will come in and be full of life, even if he's tired. He can be up for three days in a row and say, "Let's go to a show." Flash would never take you on no boat ride or to no Coney Island. Silky doesn't have to buy you nothing. He gives of himself.

Silky's just very charming. He can sweep a bitch right off her feet. When we were going to a show the other night, he kissed me on the neck and said, "This is all game." Little things like that just get me.

It's just sometimes he lets things slide. Like he calls us all down to his apartment and scares us to death. He gives us a big lecture: "I don't want you to talk to each other. I don't want this he say-she say shit. The first person who comes in this house with under two hundred dollars, I'm going to throw her out the window. You have a choice. You can leave and find yourself another fellow. Or you want your ass kicked, come home with no money." Everybody's sitting there shaking.

The first night we're scared. We're so scared we don't make no money. I call him up and he says, "How much did you make?"

"Only a hundred dollars."

He says, "Bitch, what did I tell you? Get over here now."

I get over to his apartment and walk in shaking. I say, "Silky, I'm sorry. I was so scared."

I start crying and he says, "Oh, baby." 'Cause he's too soft. If he would stick to his guns and say, "Bitch, I told you to do this, and this is what I want you to do." But he lets us get away with murder.

He tells me and Linda not to talk to each other and we do. He tells us, "Next person who runs off is going to be made an example of." That week, all of us run off. I leave. Linda leaves.

Linda goes and checks into the Holiday Inn and calls Silky and says, "I left. I'm in the Holiday Inn. Room 1621." That's how Linda leaves. Silky doesn't do nothing.

When Sandy and me first got with Silky, he was cool and hard. Sometimes he acts the old way with us, because we knew the old Silky. He treats the new ones different. Better than me and Sandy. If Silky's away from Linda's house for a while, she's so happy to see him, she may cry and say, "I missed you so much."

He don't come to see me for weeks and then I say, "Hi." I don't ever say, "I'm so happy to see you, baby." Silky doesn't think I have any feelings. I don't want him to know how I feel. If he's ignoring me deliberately, I don't want him to get the satisfaction of knowing he's succeeding.

Silky really hates to fight a girl. He doesn't even know how to. But he still thinks it's part of being a pimp. If he puts his hand up to Linda, she starts crying and shaking. He'll stop. I won't cry. I holler and curse him. Silky thinks I like to be treated badly. He thinks I'm a masochist. He used to beat me up all the time. Like if he didn't hit me for a month, I'd say, "You know, you haven't beaten me up for a while."

He says, "Is that what you want?"

I says, "No." But he's thinking that's what I want.

Silky never hits me for no reason. He hits me when I'm wrong. If he hit me for no reason whatsoever, I would leave him. You have to do a lot of things wrong to make him mad. He lets things pile up and, even then, if you're having a good time together, he may just leave well enough alone. He won't mention anything. Just to save the confusion of a fight. Just to leave me be happy.

If he was cold-blooded, he wouldn't be Silky. He walks around saying, "I'm too sweet. That's what's wrong with me." Sometimes he says, "You're going to turn me into a dirty old pimp again." I do prefer Silky when he dominates.

I feel very dependent on Silky. I feel helpless. I'm scared that I might be so totally dependent on him I won't be able to do things for myself. What do I have? With him, materially, I have an apartment and the clothes I wear. But I'm paying for this myself. He keeps telling me, "Bitch, if you leave me, you won't be nothing. You'll be a bum. How could you make it on your own?"

I say to myself, "Silky, the money I give you is what's making these things possible for me. For every dress you buy me, you get five five-hundred-dollar suits." He puts it in my head that I can't make it without him. I'm really believing him.

When I leave him after a fight, I might have four hundred dollars. I check into a hotel. Less the money I pay for the hotel, I buy a few things and when my money runs out, I call Silky. I'm basically lazy. I have to have a pimp to make money. If I'm by myself, I make just enough to get by. I don't have nothing. If I go to jail, I don't get out. If I get sick for a couple of weeks and my rent's due, I can't pay it. With Silky, I have financial security. He takes care of those expenses. I can't save money on my own, because I know I can make it again tomorrow.

Lexington and 49th is my corner. I've been on this corner longer than any other girl. It's the only place I've ever worked. I know everyone in the whole area—every hotel owner, house detective, bellman and elevator operator. I know every cop on the street.

Silky and me pass Park and 49th and I look over to Lexington. He says, "Can't stand it? Can't stand being away from home, can you?" I know every crack in the sidewalk. I know every brick in the walls. I know every nook and cranny where I can go to hide from the cops. I can run into the drugstore where they'll put me behind the counter. The cops come in, search the place, think I must have gone out the back door, and go onto the street again. I'm safe on Lexington and 49th. It's home.

Every guy knows he can find a girl on Lexington and 49th. If I go with three or four guys a night, two or three of them I've

seen before. Like Ralph. He finds me standing by the lamp-light. Sometimes I wear my hair different and he doesn't recognize me. He says, "Do you know Kitty?"

I say, "Yea, but she's out of town. Do you want to go with me?"

"No, I like Kitty."

I start to tease. "Why don't you come with me? Is Kitty cuter?"

"Yea."

"Is she nicer than me?"

"Yea, she's nicer than you. There's nobody like Kitty." I say, "Well, I am Kitty."

"How can you prove it?"

"Come home with me. I'll show you the tatoos on my titties." That's the way I prove I'm Kitty.

Usually I can't stand tricks. When you're turned out, pimps put that in your head. "You don't get off with tricks." Tricks are tricks—that's how they got their name. When they turn around and satisfy you, you're the trick. And tricks ain't shit.

Some tricks can be useful. I got a trick who's in the carpet business. I can get a carpet for cheaper and fuck most of it off. But I don't do too much bartering, because you give up cash, and if Silky don't want me to have something, I can't have it.

It's sex with tricks I hate. Sex is horrible. Just horrible. I used

to be able to stand it, but now I close my eyes and keep thinking it's a dog fucking me. It's just disgusting. If I didn't have a strong mind, I would go off—crazy. I guess with girls sex is emotional and with men it's physical. A man can put it in a Coke bottle and come.

My guys have to have pretty straight tastes. If they want to do something stupid, I won't do it. Anything other than fucking is stupid. I won't let men touch me. Or suck my titties. Hell no.

When I get a guy up to the apartment, I get the money and then I light a cigarette and put it in the ashtray. I clean the guy off and fuck. When the cigarette burns out, I know the time is up.

I see about five guys a night—the price depends. One might spend seventy-five and another forty. Ralph spends thirty-five —a bargain because he's regular.

I don't always fuck. Sometimes I just french. But that makes your teeth rotten. If it drips and gets in your gums, your mouth rots. My doctor told me that. I'm just getting to be one unhealthy bitch. I'm in the doctor's office every week with something —an irritated womb, a swollen vagina. What ruins me is having sex with Silky after I have sex with the tricks. I hurt. He's really big and good. Then I go to work and have it with six guys and get irritated.

Sometimes I go over to Silky's house after work and say, "You know, I must have fucked a hundred guys. What do you think about that?"

He says, "How much did they spend?" Shit like that he says.

Silky puts all of us down to make him be really great. He intentionally criticizes us so we blame ourselves. He doesn't ever take the blame. He constantly tells me, "No, you're wrong. You're a stupid little bitch." He's so smart and I need him. I'm dumb and ugly and Silky's the only one who will take me. I need his brain. I better stay with him forever.

Silky tries to mold me into Silky's lady. He tries to make me be what he wants. He cares about appearance. I used to wear wigs all the time. Silky stopped me. He likes natural-looking girls. All his girls are just plain girls. Fellows walking down the street can't even tell we're working.

Silky's trying to change my whole personality into Silky. That's why I'm fighting him. You talk to Sandy and you can tell she's with Silky. The way she talks, the way she moves. Linda's the same way. When Silky can tell a girl is going to stay, he works on her. He makes her him. I'm the only oddball. I just

don't want to be a robot. I don't want to be Silky. I want to be Kitty.

This is the problem. Silky is the best pimp around. I've looked at them all. I have to have a pimp, because I could never get adjusted to another life. I don't want nothing else. I feel I'm higher than other people. I'm better. I broke all the rules. I don't care if I go to jail. I just don't go along with what's supposed to be. You're not supposed to be a prostitute. You're not supposed to sell your body. But being a prostitute makes me enough money to do what I want to—be in this life.

A pimp has it better in the life than a prostitute. A pimp is better than a prostitute. He doesn't go around selling himself. My little brother was coming up and I said to Silky, "Try not to act like a pimp around him. I don't want my brother to know what I do."

He says, "I tell my family what I do."

I says, "Silky, if I were a man and I were a pimp, I'd tell my family too. I'd say, 'Yeh, I got six girls and they're out there selling it for me. All those bitches give me all their money.' I would say that. But to say I'm selling my body and after I get through selling my body, I'm giving all my money away. No."

I says, "If you were whore and you sold your body for money to a nigger, would you tell your family?"

He says, "No. I guess I wouldn't." That shows a pimp is better than a whore.

I wouldn't be with no other man but Silky. It's just that he doesn't keep his promises. Everything he promises to do with me, he never does. He does them with Linda. Silky promised to take me to *The Great White Hope*. Next thing I know, Linda's talking about *The Great White Hope* her and Silky went to see. He promises to come over and he lands up at Linda's. Little things like that. It really bugs me. Then he wonders why I'm jealous.

Look at the coats we got for Christmas. Linda's was all mink and mine was ninety percent leather. Sandy's is leather. Who's at Silky's house the most? If I'm there, Linda is there. He thinks she's "Miss-Fucking-Do-Right."

LINDA

All my girls are stars, *Silky comments,* but Linda's needed more of my time to become the kind of woman she is now. I did it for her. Not for a purpose, but because I enjoyed her. I did the same thing with Sandy. I would have done the same thing with Kitty, but she'd act crazy if I paid attention, so I stopped. Kitty can't accept attention. If I be over with her all the time, she'd start acting up. If I don't go over, she's unhappy too.

Linda is a bad bitch. I ain't a gushy fellow, but she's pretty and she's sweet. I enjoy doing everything with Linda. She's fragile and delicate and fun.

I didn't like Silky when I first met him, *Linda says*. He didn't like me either. My friend Lois and I came to New York for a weekend last October. We were at the Open End night club. Lois started talking to a fellow she'd met before and I was having an argument. I'd just left a pimp, and one of his friends was at the club. He starts yelling that I should go back to my man. I wasn't going, but he said he'd kidnap me. All of a sudden, Silky pulls up in his car and Lois and another fellow get in. So I got in too. I didn't know where I was going, but Lois knew the other guy, so I figured it was all right. Silky was my savior.

I thought Silky was handsome, even though his hair was horrible. He was so quiet and reserved. He didn't seem like no fun. We were driving around for five hours and I didn't say anything at all. Finally we went to a private night club in Connecticut and then back to his apartment.

I didn't want to have sex with Silky. I waited till he got into bed. I thought he was asleep. Then I climbed in with half my clothes on. He said, "Need some help getting undressed?" I didn't answer. He just helped me. Silky took me in about ten different positions. We went twice and then he wanted to do it again, but he couldn't get his dick hard. I said, "Forget it."

He said, "No, I can't forget it." That was the first time it ever, ever happened to him. He'd been blowing coke. Usually Silky can fuck and come and fuck and come. After that, he stopped blowing coke for months.

The next night was the Players' Ball. Silky wanted me to go, but I wouldn't. I hadn't chosen and thought if I went to the ball, he'd think I was his. The ball is very important to pimps. It's held in a club, and a committee picks the "Player of the Month." Silky was chosen. He had six white women and his Eldorado and he'd been making very good money. He's certainly one of New York's biggest pimps. Maybe the most successful. But that didn't impress *me*. I was only going to stay for the weekend.

I stayed for two weeks and we went out every single night—to clubs and after-hours spots. Silky didn't get me through sex. When we spent time together, we had fun. That's why I began to like him. Then I chose.

But I didn't give him any money. He didn't ask and I never

give him money unless he asks. I'm funny that way. I like to feel the money I make is mine—for as long as I can.

I just drifted into the life about a year and a half ago. All my good friends had gone to college, but I took a regular office job. I was bored and started hanging around black fellows. Then I met a pimp. I got to like him. This is the way they get you. First they make you like them—personal. Then they tell you stories. "You don't have to have a routine nine-to-five job. You'll have minks and diamonds. You'll have me."

Once you like the guy, he tells you he's having money problems. This guy tried to persuade me to turn a trick for two months. I'd just begun blowing reefer. I don't think I'd have ever been able to turn a trick if I hadn't been smoking. 'Cause when I started, I'd go to bed with a guy and feel awful. But right afterwards, I'd smoke and feel happy and high. I'd forget what I'd done. I also didn't have to work hard. I only turned a couple of tricks a week. Pimps outside the East are much more relaxed than New York pimps. They don't make you work every minute. You can spend something on yourself. But I began to lose respect for my fellow, because he left me alone and let me do what I wanted. I ran off. That was when I met Silky.

I never thought I would work the streets. I've always been a square girl in the life. I never think of myself as a prostitute. During the day, I play the square role. Sandy and Kitty are always whores. But I go straight in the daylight. If you work at a madam's or off a phone, you're out of the public eye. But on the street, people know what you're doing. They pass by and say, "There goes a prostitute." All of Silky's girls work the streets and he won't make no exception. There is no other way to be with Silky.

I do want to be with him. He is very attractive and charming. I like being with him. He takes me out a lot. Sometimes we do nothing. Sometimes he takes me to dinner and a show. Silky likes all his women to an extent, but I'm treated better. I get to see more of Silky. I get away with more.

If I buy a dress, he never says anything. He doesn't hit me. If I don't make any money, he doesn't ask why. He does call me his "Sometimes-Money-Making-Ass," but that's a joke.

Silky likes to show me off. One time we pulled into a gas station just ahead of another pimp friend of his. He says, "Now, Linda, get out of the car and make like you're going into the station and walk right by Joe Joe's car. Flash a little." I had to walk right by the car. Silky was laughing away. "You look good, even though you're not."

I like being seen with Silky. I like the way he looks. I like the way we look together. I know he's proud of my looks. I'm his "square girl." Kitty and Sandy look like whores no matter what. They act like whores too. They don't have nothing else. I've kept up with my old friends and I guess a little "square" rubs off on me. Silky likes it 'cause I'm not so obvious. I give him style. But sometimes I think I'm just another one of his material things—like a piece of jewelry. I'd like to be his car. He gives that car more attention than any of his girls—including me.

Of all his ladies, Silky makes it obvious that he likes me best. Silky feels specially about me. That makes me feel special. He's not supposed to show his feelings. We're a family and we're supposed to be equal. But he can't control himself. He shows a preference for me. That makes me feel honored. Silky cares about me and he doesn't hide it. I feel an obligation to him, because he's entrusted me with his feelings.

Every night, I'm down at his apartment. He doesn't make me go to work. We just spend all our time together. Sometimes I wonder whether I could ever be with another pimp after Silky. I'd have to be his favorite—not necessarily his first woman, but he'd have to prefer me. I'm spoiled. Silky's one of the best pimps around. I need to belong and Silky gives me a feeling that I have a place. With other fellows, you're just one of the girls.

Silky is so wonderful. We're so close together. We don't talk much, but then we really don't have to. He knows me and I know him. Just being together is all we need. I won't say it isn't sex. Silky is great in bed. But I love him because he's so funny and charming. Silky can sweep a bitch right off her feet.

I am not jealous with Silky. Everything he does shows he prefers me. It's hard for me to understand why the other girls stick. If I were in their position, I'd go in two seconds. Sandy he doesn't see for a week. Sometimes it's even a month. And Kitty. Well, she gets beaten everytime she sees Silky. He's never touched me. But Kitty's the kind of girl who invites violence.

I wanted Silky to give me a ring like his for my birthday. But Kitty started this rumor going around that Silky and I got married. Now Silky says he can't give me a ring like his, because then people would say we really did get married. It's all Kitty's fault.

Pimps aren't supposed to talk with one lady about another. But Silky confides in me. He's told me I'm the only healthy bitch he has. Kitty—she used to have problems with girls, but Silky hopes that's over. I don't really know, because I've read some love letters she gets from girls and I've seen the cards she writes. "I can't wait to see you and walk together holding hands in Central Park."

Sandy—she gets panicked about being old and not having anything. That's what worries her. Sandy resents me for being the favorite. She always tries to undercut me. She makes little remarks. Every opportunity she has to tell something on me, she does.

I had an argument with Sandy a couple of weeks ago. I'd just gotten out of jail and I'd been over at Silky's and wanted to get some sleep. A friend of Sandy's apparently phoned me with a date, but I don't even remember talking to her. So Sandy phoned up Silky and told him I wouldn't work. Then she called me and screamed, "If I can work all day and all night, so can you."

I said, "I do work all day and all night." We yelled and argued. But I've never tried to do anything to Sandy. Even though I know she was involved with a policeman. She'd gone out with him a few times when Silky was out of town with me. The cop wasn't a trick. He was white. Silky heard something about it and said he was going to kill Sandy. But she convinced him the cop was a trick.

I don't think Silky loves Sandy. Not the way he's in love with me. Silky doesn't have to say he loves you. Usually you're his woman without love.

Last October my aunt came up for the weekend and me and Silky took her out for dinner. Silky really charmed her and my aunt liked him. Except for he's black. She said, "Can't you find a nice white boy?"

After we dropped her off, Silky and me went out. That's the first time he said he loved me. Before he'd joked and hinted. He kept saying, "Pimps aren't supposed to fall in love." That night, he said right out, "I love you." He said, "You have something that no one else has—me. Either utilize it or destroy it. You have me completely." He tells everyone else to make money.

The first time I told Silky I loved him was at Christmas when I got my mink coat. When my aunt first saw the coat, she thought I shouldn't accept it. "It's too expensive a present to take." But now she thinks I have a pretty good deal. Last time she was here, I kept running down to Silky's house to get money to take her out. She thinks he helps me financially. I don't think she knows what a pimp is. Silky always wears his diamonds and drives that car when my aunt sees him. But we told her he was in entertainment—a vice-president of Stars Un-

limited—and I worked as a model for him.

When I talked to her the other night, she said I should stay with Silky if I loved him. Even my uncle's gotten adjusted to me having a black man. My aunt doesn't see any reason why I shouldn't stay with Silky—at least till he gets my mink coat out of storage.

I told Silky my aunt wanted to know what his intentions were. I was sitting in the bathtub and we'd been joking. He asked me what kind of dowry my family would put up. Then he asked me if I really wanted to get married. Maybe he was kidding, because he got worried and said, "You won't tell anybody I asked you?"

Silky is the first man I've ever been emotionally involved with. He makes me feel like a woman. He makes me feel wanted and needed. I've got so caught up with him. His mother wants him to settle down, and Silky keeps talking about having children. He has a big plan. He wants me to have a baby now. He said I'd have to tell the other girls that I didn't tell him I was pregnant till it was too late for an abortion—that I tricked him. I'd like to have a little Silky. But I wouldn't have a baby now.

I'd still be working and you shouldn't have a baby when you're a whore.

Silky promises to take care of me in my old age. He'd give me a business—a mod boutique with stylish clothes. Something I'd enjoy. I'd only have to work from nine to five and get that money to him. He'd deduct money to pay my food and rent. I want to get married, but I don't know whether Silky will ever get married. If he does, it won't be for a long time. I don't know whether I can wait. Right now, his mother thinks I'm bad for him professionally. Pimps aren't supposed to fall in love. I hurt his business.

SPRING

A BOAT RIDE

Silky: [Sings] I'm in love with you, baby. [Says] For real. I love you baby. Catch it?

Linda: I love you, Silky. You're lucky. My horoscope says I'm kindness itself. Kind and sympathetic.

Silky: But sometimes you're a pain in the bleep. Me. I'm affectionate. Oratorical. Shallow. Stimulating.

Linda: Here's to your stimulation!

Silky: To money.

Linda: No, to love . . .

As a professional pimp, I treat all my women equally, *Silky claims*. But my feelings for each woman differ. Sandy is the closest to me. We have the deepest and best understanding. I trust Sandy. I wouldn't go so far as to say I was in love with her. But she's earned my respect.

I'm also a human being. I bleed. I sweat. I feel. I definitely do have a preference among my women. I do have a favorite. There is not a position for a favorite in the ranks. But it occurs. It's just automatic. A mother loves all her children, but she prefers one. You have a closet full of shoes and one favorite pair. Linda is my favorite.

Linda and I are more compatible. We enjoy each other. I am in love with Linda. She's a hell of a girl. Plus, seventy-five thousand a year. She's everything. She's beautiful. She's dedicated. She's close to being perfect. I hear she lacks a little maturity. Some of my other ladies say she talks "he-say, she-say." I don't see that. And I don't hear it. To me, she's perfect.

I'm sure that Linda hates her work. It's not the thing for a sweet little girl to like. If she started liking the work, she wouldn't be the girl that I love now. Because of my program, I have to sacrifice the girls for a certain length of time. Then I retire them and give them a business. It would be dangerous for me to have a girl that didn't work. I preach against it. But I have plans for Linda to retire. She knows them. She can have her own boutique—with conservative mod clothes—the way she dresses. I don't think too far into the future, but Linda's one girl I might marry.

KITTY

Silky's crazy in love with Linda, *Kitty confides*. He's so in love, he doesn't even know how in love he is. Linda's going to ruin Silky. If he'd get his dick out of her and pay more attention to business, he might do better. I used to think Silky wanted money more than anything else in the world. Now it's "Miss Fucking-Do-Right."

I have a hatred in me on Linda. We compete with each other. Silky makes us. He's always doing little things for Linda. Things that make me jealous. Everything I tell Linda, she tells on me. We're always fighting. I call up Silky and talk him into seeing me. Then Linda calls and says she has to see him. Silky sees Linda.

Last week, Silky took me and Linda and sat us down next to each other on the bed. He beats us and slaps us at the same time. Then Silky says, "Now why are you jealous of her, Kitty?"

"Because you make me jealous. She's with you all the time."

"But Linda calls and says, 'Can I clean house?' and I says, 'Come on down.' "

I says, "She's down there all the time and I don't have a chance to offer. By the time I call, Linda's already cleaned your kitchen and the whole damn apartment."

When I first got with Silky, I'd see him every day, because I was the worst girl he had. I was always getting into trouble. He'd come over and talk to me. "Kitty, why are you doing this? One of these days, you're going to be good. I can see it in you." Instead of building me up to make money, Silky built me up to be with him as a woman. I was really good and tried hard to do everything he told me. I didn't complain about nothing. I wouldn't even call him on the telephone. I figured, if he wants to call me, he knows my number. So I never called. He never called me. He even forgot my number.

119

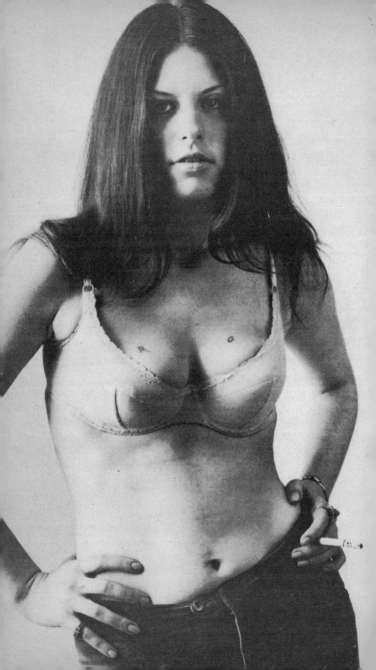

Now if he doesn't see me for a week, I go crazy. First I call him up and joke: "My face is breaking out. If you don't come and see me soon, I'm going to be ugly and then I won't make money." If he still doesn't come, I start being bad again. I complain and say, "Come and see me."

He'll say, "I'll come and see you when I want to, bitch. I do what I want." Then I do something wrong and he comes over and hollers at me and beats me up. If he beats me up on Thursday, he'll definitely be at my house Friday morning. The worse you act, the more you see Silky. Unless you're Linda.

I call Linda and say, "When are you going out to work tonight?" She don't say nothing. I say, "I'll be out around eleven."

Linda says, "Silky's taking me out to dinner. I don't know if I'll go to work."

I says, "I don't want to work either. But if Silky finds out I didn't, he'll be over on my ass." I'm boiling mad now.

Linda says, prissylike, "See you, Kitty." I just slam the phone. Linda don't work. Linda don't make no money. She's with Silky every minute. She ain't no whore, she's his mistress. She's tricked him. She's turned him away from pimping. She don't do nothing right and she has him all the time.

Sandy does everything right and what does she have—a fur coat that isn't all fur, a few diamonds, a dinky apartment. She never sees Silky. She makes no demands. She waits till he comes over. That's never.

SANDY

I'm friends with my wives-in-law, *says Sandy*, but some girls can't handle sharing their man. They speak to each other about personal things between Silky and them. If you're sharing a man, obviously you're in love with him and you don't want to hear about somebody else being with him. It's hard enough to share.

Every day, one girl or another comes to tell me something. I say, "Look, that doesn't bother me. I don't care what you do with Silky. I don't care what Linda does. All I care about is what I do. You're still out of place talking to me this way. You're not respecting me. I don't even want to hear you."

Kitty calls me all the time. She feels that talking to me is like talking to Silky, but I'm a girl, so she can talk more freely. Silky can upset her. Kitty calls and says, "What if I leave? If I leave, I leave with nothing. My apartment is Silky's, my furs and diamonds are Silky's."

I say, "Why do you think about leaving?" Every girl goes through a stage where she thinks about leaving.

Kitty gets upset because Silky spends time with Linda. She says, "How come I never see Silky, and Linda's down there all the time?"

I say, "Linda goes down there. She just goes. I'm not like that. You're not either. We're proud. Neither of us are going to call up and ask to see him, so we have to suffer. If you want to go, all you have to do is call and ask."

Kitty tells me all my wives-in-law hate me, because Silky uses me as an example of the perfect wife. I know the girls resent me, but, to tell the truth, I don't know any of the girls that well and they sure don't know me. In order to have a relationship with Silky, you've got to keep your personal business to yourself. You cannot talk to other wives-in-law about him. We refer to ourselves as a family, but we're really not. If we talked

122

openly, there would be too much jealousy. The whole game
would fall apart.

Kitty is very jealous of Linda, because she talks to her and
hears about Linda's life with Silky. I feel jealous sometimes,
but I have ways of handling it: I take a walk in the park with my
dog. Linda isn't under my skin all the time. Silky does favor
her, and Kitty knows this. Silky will always care about other
girls more than me. I accept this, because I have his respect.

Three years ago, I left Silky once, and that was because *I* let
him down. I'd been with him for just five months and he allowed me to go to Las Vegas to work. He'd never let a girl do
that before. I messed up. I didn't make any money out there.
He called and told me he needed money. I said I had it. I didn't.
Don't ask me how I got to Los Angeles, but I called him from
L.A. and he said, "Where are you?"

I said, "In L.A."

He said, "You've got to be kidding. You're crazy." He hung
up.

So I went home to Washington and stayed with my girl
friend. Sure enough, he came down after me. He called Jean
and said, "Where's Sandy?" Jean said, "She's in New York,
and if she wasn't, I wouldn't tell you where she was anyway."
He left, but he stayed around Washington.

I worked for a week and a half and put together a thousand dollars. Then I called him. He said, "It's about time you called. You're a little late." He came and got me. Sometimes I think he's wanted to beat me up, but he can hurt me much easier with words.

I've never tried to leave again. I've gained Silky's respect by standing by him. I've been through a lot for Silky. Everytime I do something for him, I just get more deeply involved.

Like the car. Silky always gets busted when he's on the road, and then I have to go and take care of it. I've had to go to Delaware on the train for that car. I've had to get a bus to some little dinky town in New Jersey.

Silky took a girl to Atlantic City for the weekend. The cops stopped him and charged him with bringing a woman into the state for pornographic purposes. They went through her pocketbook and found a douche bag. I would have said: "Your wife doesn't take a douche? Any woman takes a douche bag when she travels. Does your wife only douche when she has sex?" The cop was trying to make Silky fight the case instead of pleading guilty. So Silky pleaded guilty. Even the judge laughed when Silky said, "I brought her over the state line to fuck her."

They kept him in jail overnight. Everyone in this little town knew they had a Negro in jail with four thousand dollars in cash and tons of diamonds. I went down with another guy in the morning. We took movies of Silky getting out of the car with the cops—so we would laugh at some future time. But we wasn't laughing then.

We got busted together in Ohio. The cops following us had radioed all over the country to see if there were any charges on the car. We had one from Atlantic City, so these two cops pulled up on either side of us, pulled out guns and said, "Get out of the car with your hands up." Dandy was driving and Silky was sleeping in the back seat with his pants unzipped. They wouldn't let him zip them up.

They found grass in my pocketbook, so they took us to this little dinky jail and put Silky and Dandy in one room and me in another. Dandy thought I'd get scared and say something—which I never do. He kept saying, "Don't worry, Sandy. Everything's going to be all right." I'd rather take the whole beat and let Silky take care of it.

The cops come into your room and say the other person told on you and you're lying. Then they go tell Silky: "We already know, because your girl friend has admitted you brought her over here to prostitute herself." I told them I'd come to visit his family. But they kept us in all day long. One cop kept talking to me like he was real friendly. I never trust friendliness. He says, "Well, how do I go about finding a nice girl like you when I come to New York to visit?"

I said, "Listen, mister, you're not kidding me. You don't think I'm nice and I don't think you're nice. Let's keep cool. Now that we have that all the way out, you can leave me alone."

Two years ago, I had a bad abortion and almost died. I was sick for about six weeks. The doctor in New York said I should go home and see my family doctor, because he knew more about my history. So I went to Washington.

Silky was doing real bad. It's hard to understand, but he didn't call me at home. All my friends were saying, "If Silky cared about you, he'd be here." My best friend had a guy who played in a band. I said, "If your guy was playing a date in Madison Square Garden and you were very sick and he knew that I was taking care of you, should he come?" She said no. So I said, "Leave me alone then."

This reasoning didn't help *me*. Silky didn't call, and, finally, when I got out of the hospital, he phoned. I says, "Yeah, you don't even care about me. Just because I'm sick and I can't work, you're not going to call me." We went through a big number and he hung up. I had to stay in bed for a month. I was really miserable without him, but I was determined that I wasn't going back.

One night I got high and went out for my first night on the town. I went home, phoned Silky, and talked to him for an hour and a half. He said, "Are you ready to come home now?" I said I didn't have any money. So he sent me money, I packed up, and everyone in Washington was down on me. But one guy who was like my brother said, "If you're going to be miserable, you might as well be miserable with him."

Silky was in a picture-taking bag. When I walked into his apartment, he had his Polaroid set up on a stand and took my pictures. We haven't had any problems since then.

My devotion makes Silky stick by me. I've earned that. It may not be love on his part, but it's loyalty and a closeness that comes from being through a lot of shit together.

Recently, there've been weeks and months when I haven't seen Silky. Maybe he does take me for granted, because he knows I'm not going anywhere, so he neglects me. Still I talk to him every day—sometimes for hours. We stay close and personal. Of course, we don't have much sex. But sex with Silky isn't personal, because you know he's having sex with all the other girls. In this business, sex becomes unimportant. It's just there. You have to do a lot of growing up to realize this.

Silky's actually very cold-blooded when it comes to sex. If somebody did something with him sexually and told another girl, he'd make that girl come down and do the same thing. That's punishment for "he-say, she-say."

You'd think if a man had a group of women, he'd have group sex, but it would be the worst thing. You shouldn't have anything to do with your wives-in-law. It's like torturing yourself.

Yesterday, Linda and me were both at Silky's apartment and I thought it would be fun if we partied. Linda and Silky were in the bedroom, and I came in and said, "Do you mind if I take off my robe?"

Linda says, "What the hell do I care if you take off your robe?" So I do. Then I get in bed with them and Linda and me both start blowing on Silky. I do it for a while; then Linda does. We keep taking turns. We must have done it for four hours. Silky's so nervous he doesn't do anything to us. Finally he comes and says, "I'm glad that's over with."

Linda says, "How come you didn't do nothing to me?"

I says, "Yeah?"

Silky says, "I didn't know I was supposed to do anything." Dumb Silky was just happy to have it over.

I would never want to have Silky to myself. He isn't that type of man. He's not used to having one girl. I tell him, "I don't think any one woman could make one man happy. Men need a strange piece every now and then."

Silky says, "That's not true." But from my point of view, I've had Silky alone and it was awful. Silky's impossible to live with when he doesn't have at least three girls. Just impossible. He's used to having a lot of money. When he doesn't, he gets uptight and moody. If you're alone in his apartment, you never get any rest. Silky can't stand seeing a girl sitting still. He wants you to clean the apartment, cook, massage him, walk the dog, and go to the bank. Then you have to work too. It's exhausting. You have no time to yourself. I'm a one-man woman, but Silky sure ain't a one-woman man.

Kitty keeps saying, "When you're forty and Silky's thirty-eight, what are you going to do? You'll be an old woman and he'll still be young." That gives me the impression that all the wives are sitting around waiting for me to get old. I'm not going to get old. I'm going to grow up gracefully. I won't be working much longer—a year or a couple of years. Then Silky will get me a beauty parlor. That's what I want. I could make good money and I'm so tired of tricks. Silky won't be in this forever. Old pimps are really ridiculous. But I'll continue to support him, even when he stops, and I don't care how many women he has or who's his favorite for the moment. I have a place in his life.

Silky and me trust each other. We have the most mature relationship either of us has ever had. I might not understand him for a minute. I might get really mad and go storming around the apartment talking to myself. Then I'll sit down and say, "I know Silky. Why did he do that?" I can reason it out and say just what he would say. I know all his answers. He's made me think like a pimp. Still, I'm a prostitute. I have the advantage of thinking like a pimp and being a prostitute. I see both sides of it. I tell him that's really unfair.

I know, for instance, that Linda may be his favorite now, but one day, there will be another, and so on. That's the way pimps are; that's the way Silky is.

I don't like to have all the answers. I don't like to know what's going to be said before it's said; what's going to be done before it's done. I like some questions to which there are no answers.

Silky: Are you all set for Las Vegas?
Sandy: I'm going to leave just before the 4th of July. There's good business on that holiday, and I don't want to miss it.
Silky: I'm going to miss you, baby. How long you going stay this time?
Sandy: A month or two [laughing] till things quiet down here. You're so busy in the summer I wouldn't see you anyway. At least, if I'm away, there's an excuse. I'll see you in the winter!
Silky: Silly baby. You're my best lady, for real.
Sandy: Hey, Lisa's going to leave her guy. She phoned and told me.
Silky: Where's she at? They already split up? There's new game.
Sandy: She hasn't left yet. But she's coming to New York to look for an apartment.
Silky: People don't get ready to split up. They just do it.
Sandy: Is that what you think? I'm sure she's getting ready.
Silky: Let's say we were going to break up. You'd call me and say, forget it. And that would be that. You've done it before.
Sandy: But that was when we were just starting. Lisa's been with her guy for seven years.
Silky: It wouldn't matter if it was twenty years. Even if it was twenty days. When you get ready, you do it. You don't discuss

it. You don't stick around for a month talking about it. Because next month you'll still be here.

Sandy: I'm just saying I think it takes a little time.

Silky: And I'm just saying if you talk about it, you're not going to do it.

Sandy: Can I say one thing?

Silky: Go ahead.

Sandy: You spend a long time with somebody, you have to have been through a lot with him. You have to be real sure of what you're doing. You don't want to do something on the spur of the moment, just because you're mad about one thing.

Silky: But if you decided to leave me, or if the situation arose where we decided to part, or if we decided it wasn't going to last any longer, you wouldn't tell your friends and discuss it back and forth. You'd do it.

Sandy: That's right.

Silky: Well, Lisa's just talking.

Sandy: At the same time, you can take time to make a decision. Maybe a year. I might be feeling like that for a whole year [laughs].

Silky: Well, tell me so I'll know.

Sandy: Oh, I could never do that. I'm just giving you an example.

Silky: You must tell me so I'm given three-hundred-sixty-five days' advance notice.

Sandy: You know the way I am. I've always thought that if I was ever to leave you, I would get some money together, I'd save some for myself, and then I'd just go. Would that be stupid? Silky?

Silky: No. You've been pimped up. You're very intelligent.

I have to spend a lot of time being a professional and working, *Silky says*. So does Sandy. I don't think she fools around with other guys. Not to my knowledge. Some girls fool around automatically. But I don't have that problem. I'd be shocked if Sandy carried on with someone else. I'd kick her out right away.

Some people say my family would fall apart if Sandy left, but she's not in charge. I am. Nothing would happen if she went. All the other girls would be glad to see her go, because they're jealous of her position. Only Kitty likes Sandy, but still she calls her "Miss-Do-Right."

I have no problems with Sandy. She depends on me. Once a year, she loses confidence in herself. I reassure her. She'll say she's too old for me. I'll say, "Of course not." She knows I'm sincere. She knows me as well as I know her. I don't think she worries about the future.

Most people in the life don't plan. They think they can always pimp and always be a prostitute. Suddenly it's all over and they have to get a job. I plan to buy businesses and get out in ten years. If not sooner.

If Sandy's by my side to help me, she'll come right along. I plan to buy her a large beauty salon. Something she would enjoy. If she continued in the business, she'd keep her phone and give her dates to the other little girls I had. She'd madam on the side. Girls who get older and stay in the life become madams; others get their own businesses. Just about every wig shop on Broadway and Seventh Avenue is owned by a former prostitute.

Some people have different feelings about how long they'll live and what they'll do with their afterlife. I have no illusions. I just try to enjoy my stay on earth as long as possible. Afterwards I'll take my medicine. If I get sent down there, I just hope I can pimp a little and I'll be happy. Me and Dandy have a birthday coming up, so I've been thinking hard.

A BIRTHDAY PARTY

Silky: Here's birthday boy.
Dandy: To you, too.
Silky: Twenty-one and I can vote.
Dandy: It's eighteen now.
Silky: You're an old chap.
Dandy: I'm a year older, but you are too. I'm sweet sixteen and never been kissed.
Silky: Right on. I've got some Coke. What's you think we're celebrating for? Coke and champagne. Kitty, get champagne for everyone.

Lois: [Kidding] Hello, wife.
Linda: Hello, wife.
Lois: Wake up, everybody.
Cindy: How are you?
Linda: Well I just got out of jail for the eighth time in two months.

Kitty: Everything in our world is vice versa. The guys get served first. They come first. Outside, men are supposed to open doors for ladies. But with Silky, *you* open the door. If there are packages to be carried, you carry the packages. Usually men take care of women, but in this situation, women take care of men. Except Linda. Silky takes care of Linda. He goes against the rules.

134

Sandy: [To herself] Poor Silky. Everything's going wrong. I feel so sorry for him. His car, he can't get out of repairs. He couldn't get his jewelry today because he was short a few hundred dollars. [To Dandy and Silky] Want to blow out all those candles?

Silky: Thank you. Ain't that sweet?

Dandy: You're growing up, young snapper.

Silky: I finally found out you were forty-three.

Dandy: You're not too far behind.

Silky: I'm far, far behind. Let's blow on 'em, tiger.

Dandy: I've gotten so far up all they had to do was put one on mine.

Silky: Blow 'em out.

Dandy: Did you make a wish?

Silky: I made three or four.

Dandy: I'm modest. I made one.

"Most of the fellows I know have great pride in pimping."

"My treats!"

KITTY

I was mad at Linda at the birthday party. She can sit around and laugh with Silky all day long, *Kitty says*. She couldn't even go out and buy Cokes. She ended up going downstairs to the machine in the basement to get orange juice. What kind of party is that?

Me and Sandy cooked all day long. We were trying all day to find some shylock so we could get the rest of the money to buy Silky's jewelry. We were up all day and had to get meat and the stove didn't work so we had to cook at someone else's house. We forgot about the cake and had to run quick and get it. Linda was asleep all day and she called and asked me to wake her up around nine or ten, so she could get dressed and go down to Silky's—while I'm sweating and cooking.

I just asked her to buy Cokes and she said, "I ain't doing it. You do it." I got really mad. Me and Linda are friends, but I'm going to start staying away from her because she upsets me. She tells me things about Silky I don't want to hear. "I saw Silky today. Did you?" Stupid things she'll be asking me. We're as good friends as wives-in-law can be, but I don't want to hear how many times she got fucked last week.

Sandy's going to work in Las Vegas for the summer. I'll miss her. When I get down, she can always cheer me up and show me the right way to think.

I've been doing really good and making money. Silky's started coming every other day. Monday we were lying in bed and I said, "How come you're seeing me so often?"

"There was a time when I used to see you every single day, remember?" In the beginning, he did.

I says, "How come you do everything with Linda?" I wouldn't care if he called me up and said, "How about a show?" and I said, "No, I don't feel like it." But he don't give me a chance to say no. I'm always hearing Linda say, "I saw

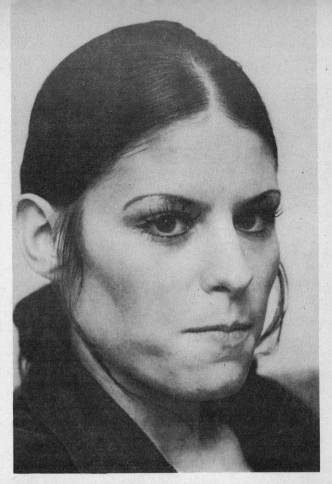

Shaft last night and it was really terrific.

So Silky says, "Kitty, you take care of your business and I'll take care of mine. You don't have to worry about no other bitch." All of a sudden, he jumps out of bed and says he's going over to wake up Linda so she can go to court, to sign a release for our bail money. He says I should hurry up and get ready and go down to court too.

I says, "I don't have to go."

"You go and take care of your own case," Silky says.

"Every time Linda has a case, I go down and take care of it for her."

"I've got to take care of my business. You go and take care of yours."

I says, "Okay." But I'm cross because I don't have nothing to do down there—just wait in a taxi for Linda to sign the court papers.

Silky's supposed to send Linda over to my place. I'm waiting and she don't come. So I go over to Linda's. I knock on her door and here is Silky laying in her bed. She isn't even ready to go to court. I says to Silky, "I thought you couldn't sleep. What are you doing over here?"

"I'm watching TV."

"Why couldn't you watch TV at my house?"

"Don't question me." I don't say nothing. I go to court and come back. I'm really mad. I call him at Linda's and say, "This is the kind of shit I was telling you about. When you jump out of my bed and go over to Linda's."

He says, "You don't know what I'm doing over here. And don't question me. Don't question nothing." I tell him to go jump in the lake. He hangs up.

I leave him, but I don't leave the apartment, so he thinks I'm still with him. The apartment is supposed to be Silky's, but I figure I've given him over two hundred thousand dollars since I've been with him, so at least I can keep this place.

Silky comes over the next morning. I have some guys here who wouldn't let nobody do nothing to me. Silky comes and rings the bell, and I says, "Who is it?" All of a sudden, Silky sees one of my guys, goes back to his car, and drives away. I says to the guy, "You know, he don't think I've left him."

The next night after I get through work, I call up Silky and he says, "I saw your little friends."

"What little friends?"

"I saw your little friends out there. I thought you'd gone."

"I did."

"What are you doing at my house?"

"It's my house."

"It's my apartment and you can't have it."

"I can't have nothing for the time I've been with you? It's mine."

He says, "Get out of it."

I says, "You can't come in my apartment."

"I'm going to get you out."

"No, you can't."

I come home from work and sleep till one o'clock in the afternoon. I hear my locks jiggling. I'm supposed to be a real sound sleeper, but I was subconsciously waiting for Silky. I

142

open the door and there's Linda with the locksmith. I say, "Look. This is my apartment. I'd appreciate it if you would get out of here."

The locksmith goes, but right behind him is Silky with Dandy. I slam the door and say, "You're not getting in." Silky tries to knock the door down with his foot, but he's in his slippers and he hurts his foot. He can't kick no more.

Dandy's talking to me through the door and Silky starts up

the fire escape outside. The cops catch him. They say, "Don't move or we'll shoot." He's swinging on the fire escape and scared to jump down because he'd hurt himself and they'd shoot him. He didn't know what to do. Finally he jumps down and the cops bring him up here. I'm running back and forth between the window and the door, because I figure Silky is still coming up the fire escape. I don't see what happened.

Silky knocks on the door, "Open up."

"I ain't opening up."

"Look out here," he says. "You're friends are here."

I look out and Jesus Christ, I thought he's brought the cops after me. I don't have my guys around, because I don't think Silky would dare do anything in the daylight. The cops say, "Open up in the name of the law" and all that shit. So I open the door and Silky starts coming after me.

I say, "Keep him away from me."

Silky says, "This is my apartment and I want her out." So Silky is fighting about whose apartment this is and whose is this and whose is that.

Silky says, "Give me my ring."

"It's not your ring. It's my ring."

"I bought it and my name is on the receipt from the jewelry store. Give it to me. Right now."

I says, "Give me my spoon." He tears his diamond spoon off and throws it on the floor and says, "Now give me my diamond ring."

I says, "I'm not going to." I'm sitting right on the bed and the cops are standing near Silky so he can't get near me. My baby's right beside me.

Silky says he pays the rent. I says I pay the rent. He says, "Get the super up here."

Last month I was late paying the rent and told the super, "I'm waiting for that man to bring me money." Silky had double-parked outside and the super saw him. Silky gave me the rent money and left. The super remembered that.

Now Silky says to the super, "Who pays the rent?"

The super says, "The girl does."

"Where's she getting the money from?"

The super says, "You. She was waiting for you to pay the rent."

Silky says, "See, officer. See where she gets the money to pay the rent?"

I says, "Yes, Silky. But you tell them where you get the money to give for the rent. And everything else."

Silky says to me, "Are you out of your mind?"

So the cop says, "Looks like you've been living here common-law and looks like the young lady's clothes are in the closet. So it looks like you're going to have to settle this in court."

Silky says, "Let me talk to her alone for a couple of minutes." The cop says it's up to me and I say no. Silky would have jumped on me right then and there when the cops left.

Silky says, "I'm not going to do anything to her. I'll go to jail for assault, right?" The cop says that's right. Dandy says he'll talk to me and I says yes, I'll talk to him.

Dandy says, "Why do you do this?"

"Don't even ask me why, Dandy. I don't even know why."

So I left Silky and I was living with another girl. I was so lonely. I missed him so much. Sandy was trying to cop me and everyone thought I was going back to the family.

I was, but Silky had just gotten circumcised, because it hurt him and he thought it would break. It was growing, I swear. I guess if you use it a lot, it gets bigger—so big the skin won't hold it. I wanted to wait till he was well. I said to Sandy, "You just let me know when he's better and I'll choose."

One night Sandy told me to wait for Silky, because he was going to buy me breakfast. She told Silky to come out on the stroll, because I'd buy *him* breakfast. So Silky pulls up in his car and I'm on this guy's motorcycle. He says, "Come over here. Where are you going?"

"Home."

"Can I join you?"

"No."

"Why not?"

"Because you won't take me home."

"If you want to go home, I'll take you straight home. But I doubt very seriously that you want to go home."

"No, I don't."

"Come on. I'll drive you. For real." So I get in Silky's car and we go through Central Park, driving around and talking. He asks me do I miss him and how I feel about being a bum. "Isn't it an awful, miserable, lonesome thing? You're nothing without me, right?" He keeps pounding this into my head.

I think, "God, I'm miserable. I'm lonesome. I can't stand it any more. I'm nothing without Silky."

He's staying in a hotel, because he doesn't want to be around girls. If he saw a girl, his cock would grow; that would hurt him, and his stitches would break. So we go to the hotel and he keeps fucking around and saying, "Will you be my woman?" He gets me all down on the bed and shit. I really want to fuck. He keeps stalling and says, "What is it, yes or no?" That turns me off. Four times he gets me really excited and then stops. Now I know why he had that self-control. He takes his fucking clothes off and has nothing on but his shorts. He's getting me excited again. Then he gets up and this big old white thing is hanging out of his pants. I says, "Oh fuck."

Two days later when he got his bandage off, I think he fucked everybody. He fucked me too.

Now I'm back with Silky. He promises to spend more time with me. Maybe one day a week. So what if Linda gets six days. I'll at least have Silky on Saturday, and Silky's all I want.

This weekend, we're going to Coney Island. We'll take my baby Betsy too. I don't spend much time with Betsy. She lives with a babysitter and I see her once a week. I can't get her to call me mother. She calls the babysitter mommy, but not me. That really hurts.

Betsy's father was a trick, *Kitty recalls*. I don't know who he was. I wasn't supposed to be able to get pregnant, so I didn't take no pills. Then it happened.

Silky almost made me give up Betsy. I'd got so dependent on him that I'd phone him about everything. I said, "Silky, do you think I should give up Betsy?"

He said, "That's your decision to make, but, if I were you, I'd give Betsy up." He got that in my head.

Betsy didn't like Silky. I think Silky didn't like her. Baby's can sense that. The babysitter thinks maybe his color bothers her. But maybe Betsy thinks that Silky is more important than she is.

148

Lately Betsy and Silky have gotten to like each other more. The babysitter was sick and Betsy had to stay one night with Silky, so I could go out to work. Betsy had a terrific time and Silky was so proud of hisself. Everytime he raised his fist in the black power sign, Betsy would say, "Right on." He thought he'd learned her that.

Silky says to me, when I walk in the door, "See what Betsy does!" He raises his fist and Betsy says, "Right on."

I says, "Oh Silky. Betsy's done that since she was a tiny baby." I really don't know what else he taught her, but she wanted to go see him the next day.

I brought her down before I took her to the babysitter. Linda was also at the apartment, lying on the bed with Silky. Silky's kissing Linda and Betsy's jealous. She keeps saying, "Kiss Kitty, Silky." So Silky tells her to get out of the bedroom and go look for all the money she can find in the apartment.

Betsy's picking up pennies in all four corners of the living room. She's very thorough about money. Then she asks me for money. I gives her a dollar. She takes another dollar from Linda's purse. Finally she gets together about three dollars and I tell her to give it to Silky and tell him she'd chose.

So she goes and says, "Here Silky. I choose."

He says, "Okay. Now out to work."

Betsy comes and tells me she has to go to work. I says, "Betsy, you go back and tell Silky you just chose and you should have your first night off."

Silky says, "You spent all last night with me, Betsy. It's work tonight."

So I says to Betsy, "How're you going to work?"

She says, "I'm going to sell p . . ." She gets stuck on the *p*. I think she's going to say pussy, and, oh shit, where'd she learn that.

I says, "Sell what, Betsy?"

Finally she says, "Potato chips."

So we're riding back in a cab and Betsy says, "I want to go to work."

I says, "You can work at the sitter's." I took her to buy some potato chips.

Kitty: Can you stay?
Silky: I've got to take care of the car. And then I've got to take a bath.
Kitty: Take a bath here. Betsy, come here. Say, "Silky." See,

151

she really likes you now. She'd like to cook you a meal.

Betsy: 'Bye.

Silky: 'Bye.

Kitty: Come on, Silky. You won't come back. You'll go to Linda. I don't want to take no chances.

Silky: I promise I'll come right back.

Kitty: Your promises ain't no good. Except to Linda.

Silky: Swear on pimp's heaven. Now cool it. Pimp's honor I'll come back.

Kitty: You won't come for another week. You'll be with Linda every day.

Silky: I'll come over tonight.

Kitty: Please stay. It will bring me bad luck if you don't.

Silky: Here's a promise.

Kitty: It's bad luck for me. I'll go to jail if I don't see you.

Silky: Come on. Go to work and I'll be here in the morning.
Kitty: You always tell me things.
Silky: I'll see you this morning. I've got to do my hair.
Kitty: I'll do it.
Silky: But you got no rollers.
Kitty: Yes, I do. Come on, Silky. If you want me to come and see you, I always come.

Silky: And if you want me to come and see you, I'll come. Want me to come and see you in the morning?
Kitty: You ought to see me right now. Come on.
Silky: I'll see you in the morning.
Kitty: You're just going to see Linda. I can't wait that long.
Silky: You'll make it. I bet you can.
Kitty: Something bad is really going to happen to you, Silky. You and that damn Linda.
Silky: That's right. Some guy's going to beat up on me. Bye-bye.

Kitty has a penitentiary personality, *Silky remarks*. She's rougher than my other girls. This is the life for Kitty. She's a down ho. If Sandy wasn't with me, she'd go right back to stripping. Kitty just wants to be a whore.
Kitty is more passionate than any of my other girls. That passion brings us close together when we're drifting apart. I'm not talking about sex. I don't think Kitty is the best lay in the world.

153

All my girls are bad. But if Kitty thinks she's best for me sexually, that's cool. That's what she's supposed to think. It holds her to me.

What I'm talking about is temperament. Kitty fights. She's trouble, but she takes care of trouble. If one of my girls gets threatened on the street or in jail, Kitty will take care of it. With her fists. Kitty would do anything for me. I expect she'd kill.

Kitty is in jail all the time. She hasn't been making any money, but you just don't throw a girl away. She's worth my attention. I just don't have any to give.

Recently, she's run away a couple of times. I haven't had time for her and we drifted apart. Then we patch up. My intentions are always to talk to the girls about what made them leave, but if I'm tired, I may just fall asleep and forget it.

Kitty is being tamed by me. I think I can make her demure and sweet.

Last week, I got picked up and had to go to jail, *Kitty says*, because Silky didn't have no money for bail. I've been in the House of Detention but I've never been to Riker's Island before. I can't describe it. It was just horrible. They don't treat you any kind of way but like prisoners.

A girl, Pat, came in with me when I was admitted. She wore drag, but I was so mad, I didn't notice. We got sent to the hospital together—to get a syphilis check. They can't put you in general population until you're cleared, otherwise you might spread something through the whole institution.

I was in a cell by myself. I didn't have anything to do but think. All I thought about was Silky. I thought about how bad he treats me and how much he loves Linda. Every day I was in jail, girls would come from off the streets and tell me what was happening. I knew Silky was in Boston. You get word faster in jail than you do in the street. One girl tells another from floor to floor. Word gets passed along. I heard that one judge gave a girl twenty-seven thousand dollars' cash bail. She was just a street girl. A girl in for murder had a seventy-thousand bond, which means about five thousand cash. For murder. And the whore gets twenty-seven thousand cash. No bail. The judge declared *her* a public enemy.

When I first went to jail, I got involved with girls. This time I met a girl who reminded me of Silky. She was real, real big. I walked into my cell and she was sitting there. I said, "What are you doing in my room?"

She said, "Take it easy. Don't be scared. I'm here and no one's going to bother you."

I said, "I know what you want from me. If this gets back to
154

Silky, he'll murder me." We never did get around to doing nothing.

Silky hates girls with girls. I could be broadminded about relationships with girls if it wasn't for Silky. The problem for a pimp is his reputation. Fellows are put down who let their girls make it. Silky's threatened by a woman having love with another woman because he can't compete. He can compete with another pimp, but how can he compete with a woman?

All of Silky's girls have a bit of lesbianism. They need a man to prove they're not. If you're with a guy, that takes away all traces of doubt you might have about yourself. Jail sets you back, because there aren't no men. I almost always get close to girls when I'm in jail.

Jail is the worst place in the world. We had to wash windows and clean the whole floor. I was the only prostitute in my section. Everybody else was junkies, and two people were up for murder. They all felt sorry for me, because they knew I was a prostitute and never did no work in my life. We had to wake up at five in the morning. Ordinarily, I'd just be getting home. The girls all joked on me. They'd tell the officer, "Poor Kitty. Ain't done no work in her life. It's bad enough the poor thing's in jail."

When they first asked me to wash windows, I said, "No. I'm going to do my time locked up. I'm not going to do no work." Finally, I decided to work. So I'm washing this window and the officer comes to tell me it's streaked and I should wash it again. I wash it again and it's still streaked, so I quit. I go to my cell and say I'm not coming out. The officer gives me an infraction.

After I've been in for a week, the officer comes and says, "Kitty, do you ever want to go home? There's someone downstairs with bail."

I says, "I don't care if I go home or not."

"That's the way it looks. It looks as though you want to stay here."

I says, "I do. I love this fucking place."

"Someone's here to pick you up. Do you want me to tell them you refuse bail?"

"Yes. Tell 'em." I thought she was fooling me into washing windows. I thought she was lying. I thought there was no bail.

She says, "I'll tell who's ever downstairs with bail that you're refusing it." She goes downstairs and comes back. "I'm going to give you one more chance. Don't you really want to go home? Someone's here. I'm serious."

"I don't want to go home. I don't care who's here. I'm not going home."

She says, "I'm going to call the captain. This is the last chance I'm giving you."

"My bail happens to be one thousand dollars in cash. I have exactly two wives-in-law in New York and I know they don't have money. My man's out of town. Most of my wives-in-law are out of town. There ain't nobody to put up bail. You're just trying to make me wash windows."

She calls the captain, and I think they're going to give me another infraction. She says, "I'm giving you one last chance. Linda Johnson is . . ."

I says, "Linda Johnson!" I thought she was bullshitting me. She says, "Linda Johnson is downstairs. Are you taking bail or what?"

I ran down the hall and told everybody to take their windows and shove it. When I heard Linda's name, I went a little crazy. That was the first time I was ever glad to hear her name.

I was going to leave Silky when I was in jail. I didn't understand why—with seven wives-in-law—I was in jail for six days. I understood after I talked to Silky. It turned out he really didn't have no money. A pimp is supposed to be in a position to take care of bail, but he can't just snap his fingers and money comes. He's got to get it from us. If we're not giving him money, he can't have no money. How could I make money when I was in jail?

I also thought about how much trouble I create. When Silky does create a little something, I make it a big deal. I always make things bigger than they are. I start shit. Maybe he doesn't love Linda. He's just caught a new girl and he's stopped seeing Linda so much. Maybe I made Linda a princess in Silky's court, because I feel like a whore beside her. Maybe *I* blew Linda up.

I decided to stop bugging Silky and we ain't had no problems since. I feel real good with him. I don't know how Silky feels about me. I still don't know when I'm going to see him. That makes it great. That makes it interesting. If I knew every day when I came home Silky would be there, we would have a boring relationship. There would be no competition. I'd turn into a fucking pig. Now I'm always trying to impress him and he's trying to impress me. That makes us like each other more. It's a big challenge. I wouldn't be happy any other way. We're all healthy, normal women. If we didn't get jealous, something would be wrong. We're all playing a game. Someone said that the world was a stage and we're all actors. I'm playing Silky's whore. I create myself. It's fun.

Of course, Silky lies to make us feel good. He tells us a differ-

ent story every time about where this will all lead. He figures out what we want to hear and then he promises.

Silky comes over to my house and he leaves. I say, "When are you coming back?" If he said, "Next week," I would go crazy. So he says "I'll be over in the morning." He's lying and he knows it. I know he's lying, but I pretend he's coming over in the morning. All night I'm real happy. I make a lot of money, because I think Silky's going to be there when I come home. He ain't.

When I talk to him, he tells me this big, fantastic story about how he couldn't get there. This little funky bitch Linda did something so he had to go and take her to a show. He keeps lying to pacify. He lies to make me happy. If Silky comes over and he can't stand me, I'm going to be upset and leave him. Instead, every time he walks out the door, he says, "Back to work. How I hate to go back to work."

I say, "Do you consider me work?"

"Did I say that? I said I have to go *back* to work." When he leaves Linda's house, he says, "Back to work. The only place I can rest is here with my baby." He sells her the same thing. All the lies he tells are lies to make us happy. They're not really lies, because, whatever he says, while he's saying it, he really means it and believes it.

Silky's whole thing is being himself. He might say the same

thing to me that he says to Linda, but that's just the way he talks. You can only think of so many things to say!

If I can put up with two more years of Silky, I can put up with him forever. In two more years, I'll be too old to start over with someone else. I don't want to live by myself. Silky does understand me. After I've been with him for three and a half years, why should I throw everything I've worked for away and leave him? I'll have at least two hundred fifty thousand dollars behind me that I will have given him. I'll have my diamonds and my minks.

I have Silky. One-seventh of him in the summer. One-third in the winter, when just the regular girls are left. I believe in Silky. Eventually, we're all going to have businesses of our own. Sandy has been with him for three years, which isn't a very long time. When she's worked two more years, Silky will say, "Sandy. You quit. That's enough selling pussy for you.". Nobody's worthy of a business now. How would it look if he said, "Here's your little shop and go run it." The time hasn't come for us.

I wouldn't want a business anyway. That's supposed to be our goal, but I'd rather be a madam for the rest of my living days. I don't want to get up at nine in the morning and sell clothes to people all day long. If Silky gets Sandy a beauty parlor, you know what kind of beauty parlor it's going to be. Sandy is not going to have her name outside and people working for her. The shop will be open from eight to eight and she'll be setting and washing peoples' funky hair.

Linda will be selling clothes to schmucks. She'll be crawling out of bed at nine and over there to open up the place and sit and sell clothes. That ain't no future.

Right now, I don't think beyond the stroll. I was saying to Silky, "Will you take me to shows when I get old?" If I stick with him and become a madam, or Silky gets me a business, will he still want me as a woman? That's what worries me. When Silky's forty, he's still going to be getting little twenty-year-old girls. If you're old, and you can have a twenty-year-old girl out selling pussy for you and you have a fifty-year-old bitch sitting around in some apartment, who're you going to want? I asked him whether he'd walk down the street with me. He said he knew a good plastic surgeon that would fix me up.

Competition ain't so tough now. Linda's the biggest competition. She tells me she's going to run away and I tell Silky. So he decides to sell Linda to a guy for a thousand dollars. This guy is going to meet Silky under a bridge outside Philadelphia. Silky gets Linda in the car and starts driving. As usual, Silky's late and the guy isn't under the bridge. Linda tells me she wasn't scared, but Silky says she was scared to death.

Silky's stopped seeing Linda as much. In spring and summer, Silky cops new girls. He likes them, because they're different. He sees what he can learn about them and figures out how long they'll stay. He can make a girl really content in the beginning. Then he stops seeing you and you go crazy.

Linda's going crazy. She calls Silky every day, demanding that he come over and see her. She'll say, "I haven't seen you in two days."

Silky says, "I haven't seen Kitty in a week. That's where I'm going." Linda gets mad. She calls him up twenty times a day when she's not with him. He's getting sick of her.

One day he got so mad, he said, "If Linda don't call me all day, I'll go see her. But I don't think she can make it." He gave her up to six to call or not to call. At about five forty, she called and blew it.

Linda's been on top and she doesn't want to lose her position. But with a new girl like Tracey, who can tell?

TRACEY

Tracey is a bad bitch, *according to Silky*. I met her at a club in Montreal, *he recalls*. She was running back and forth to the ladies' room, so I knew she was interested in me. I said, "There's a real one in town."

I thought Tracey was a little cutie pie. When I first saw her, I wasn't sure she was in the life. But after I got to know her, I realized she was.

She's a Gemini like I am, but she's not as stable as me. She's young and restless and inexperienced. She sees other girls running free and wants to skip up the street too. She doesn't know New York and she wants to sight-see. I ask my women to work seven days a week. They don't have free time.

But Tracey's twin sister has a chump. He lets her do anything and everything she wants—she works from twelve to two five days a week and goes shopping every afternoon. That makes Tracey look like a prisoner.

There are easier conditions for the girls. Some pimps don't pimp, but then they don't have anything. They live in a hotel with two changes of clothes. If that's what you want for selling your pussy, you can have it.

A girl who comes to me can build a future. I try to tell Tracey. I'm established—with cars and jewelry, apartments, and closets full of clothes. The strong survive in this life. The weak fall by the wayside—with nothing.

Tracey says, Silky's the sixth pimp I've been with in a year. Usually I stay for two weeks and get bored. Silky just said to me, "Do you think we have a lifetime together?"

I said, "I don't know."

He says, "How long have we been together?"

"Six weeks."

"What's the longest you've ever been with a guy?"

I said, "About two months."

160

"Do you think we'll make it?"

I said, "I'm not going to make any promises I can't keep."
Then he made me promise to stay with him for two months.

I'd been living with my family in Ottawa. They don't mind
me being in the life. When I got busted in Ottawa, I lost my
phone, so customers used to phone me at home and I'd go out.
My mother would see the guys pick me up. She knew they were
tricks. I think if she were my age, she'd do this. She saw all the
money I had and how much fun my work was. Like I really
didn't have to work for my money.

My father makes good money—about six dollars an hour as a
manager in a plant. Three years ago, my friend Peter would get

stolen things and my dad would sell them. The police caught my father with about two hundred stolen suits in a closet in our house. So my father had to go to trial. Then he was out on probation. He's a little bad himself.

One Sunday morning, I left for Montreal, where my twin sister Trixey was living with her man. Trixey and me went out that night. I didn't hardly know anyone. We went to this bar and I saw a guy and said, "Trixey, who's that?" Trixey didn't know. I walked to the washroom and passed him and he said, "There's a real one in town." I turned around, looked at him, and went back to my table. The bars were about to close. It was two minutes to three. So I walked past that fellow again and he said, "Pretty. Pretty." I thought, he's a doll. Who is he?

He wore a brown pinstriped suit with a short jacket and that special hat. I says, "What's your name?

And he says, "Silky."

I says, "I know you. I know Linda."

I spent the night with him, but we didn't do anything. We fooled around—kissing and holding. I was supposed to phone him the next day, but I forgot his room number. (You never know a guy's last name!)

In the evening, I was at the Penthouse Club and he walked in. I said, "I forgot your room number."

He says, sarcastic, "Sure." He walks to the bar and I think, shit, he's going to be cool. I wanted to say, "I'm sitting with friends and if you want to talk to me, call tomorrow." But I really wanted to go to bed with him. In Ottawa, you could go to bed with pimps before you chose. With New York pimps, no.

Finally we went home together to his place at the Holiday Inn. That was where it happened. I didn't choose him, but I had sex with him. Before I met Silky, sex just wasn't like this. No man went into all these different positions. When I was with other guys, it was just up and down. Silky sat up and did it facing me. He puts your legs up real high, and I'm very small inside and he's very big. Men and women come in different sizes. Small, medium, and large. If a girl's small she need medium. This time I got large, but, even though it hurt a little, it was real exciting. Silky comes at you from every side; he's a good lover —that's for sure.

When I first came to New York with Silky, we went directly to Sandy's house. He says, "She's my main lady." Then he says, "Not my main." You're not supposed to talk about a girl as the main lady. He did give Sandy a kiss right in front of me.

I'd like to have Sandy's relationship with Silky. Sundays he goes to Sandy's. Once a week. He said, "The best girl I've ever known is Sandy. Sometimes she gets sentimental because she's in love." Then he stopped. He forgot he was talking about another lady.

When Sandy was going to the Diamond Exchange to get her watch, I was sitting in the car between Silky and Sandy. He leaned over, gave her a kiss and said, "Happy third anniversary." Then he turned to me and said, "How long have we been together?"

I said, "About a month." He gave me a kiss too, because he felt my reaction.

A pimp and a whore aren't supposed to be in love. Maybe Silky is in love with one of his girls. Maybe Linda. But from what I see, she puts herself in a position to make me think that she's the favorite. It would probably bother me if I *really* thought Silky had a favorite, but I don't feel he does.

Silky's been training me. He says, "If I could get the teen-age kid out of you, you'd be okay. You're a snob. You're stuck up."

I say, "Tell me what I do wrong."

He says, "I'll tell you when you do something wrong, but I can't tell you offhand."

I used to give Silky mouth. In Ottawa you could tell pimps shit. I've learned not to talk back to Silky. Sometimes I fool around. I might even be serious, but I do it in a joking manner. I say, "I'm not going to stay in your apartment cleaning shit all day."

He says, "Remember. You're on the *seventeenth* floor." I have to be careful. I can't say what I want. I don't talk to Silky about my problems. It's always on the light level. Sometimes we'll dip into something personal, but not that deep.

Like Silky doesn't want me to leave the house unless I ask him. I think that's very foolish. I feel like a prisoner. If he wasn't home and I didn't go to work and then told him I wasn't supposed to leave without his permission, he would kill me. It would be funny, but he wouldn't take it that way.

I don't like being tied down. I say, "Listen, Silky, I don't want to ask for permissions. I'm not a little girl. It's worse than when I was twelve and had to ask my parents for everything. Like if I wanted to go to the store. Some girls like this, but I don't. It doesn't make me come in my pants."

Silky thinks I should enjoy doing things for him. I don't like setting his hair. I used to do that every day and complain. Now I just do it. I find Silky very spoiled. Like all this shit about

164

massaging him and washing his back. I'm not used to it. Maybe because I never lived with a man before. Last week, he asked if I felt like a wife to him. I said, "Shit, no!"

I'm kind of shy with Silky. Maybe because I'm in this business. Or maybe because I've never been able to open up to Silky. I don't say nothing when we lay down or when we're having sex. I don't say "I love you," or even tender or dirty things.

I'd like to say I love you, but it's not there yet. When you're having intercourse with a guy you like, you get involved and your like turns to love. You want to express yourself. I couldn't say, "I like you, Silky," because he'd say, "Look bitch, I want you to love me." We were going to Atlantic City and I was sitting up front in the car. Kitty and Linda didn't like this, 'cause I was sitting beside Silky.

This song came on and it said, "You're going to get my love." Silky said to me, "I'm going to get your love."

I said, "Oh no you won't."

He said, "Yes I will."

I'd really like to say, "Baby, you feel good." I can't even say that. I guess it's getting better now, because before I never even thought of saying it. I didn't think Silky cared, so I couldn't get into him. But last night. Wow! He usually doesn't kiss on the

lips. That turns me on—affection. This time he kissed me and aroused me more than ever before. He wouldn't just come out and say, "I dig you." He said, "You're not hard to like, Tracey. For real." Any girl would like her guy to say, "Baby, I love you."

I was telling Silky that all his ladies talk about me behind my back. He says, "Tracey, don't you realize they're probably jealous of you." I'm living with Silky. Sandy is the only other girl that's ever lived with him and that was when they were just beginning and he couldn't afford another apartment for her. Linda's really jealous.

Silky and me made an arrangement in Montreal. He said I only had to work six days a week. One Sunday night, I'm sitting at Silky's relaxing and Linda walks in before she's going to work.

She says, "How come you're sitting around in your robe? Aren't you supposed to go to work?"

I says, "I have Sundays off." So Linda goes running into the bedroom where Silky's asleep and screams, "You let that bitch work only six days a week and all the rest of us are out there every night."

Silky came and told me to get dressed and go to work. Since Linda made that trouble, I've had to work on Sundays too.

Linda told Silky I was going to run off just so he'd beat me. I thought he was going to kill me. He hit me in the face with his hand. I put my hand up trying to protect myself. I fell on the floor and then he told me to get up and made me take more. There was blood on the wall where I fell. What really hurt was Linda sitting there when he told me to wash the wall. He says, "You wash every wall in the apartment. I don't want nothing dirty except you."

That night I went to work and never came back. The next night, Silky picked me up off the stroll. It was exciting. I felt wanted. I didn't know what was going to happen. But I felt he cared enough to come and get me. He said, "What did you leave for?"

"Oh Silky. I'm so sorry." I put on a little-girl act—trying to get sympathy so he wouldn't beat me again. I says, "I want to stay with you, Silky. But I'm so scared of you."

He says, "I was so mad. I don't like beating my ladies." I pull a little sucking act so he won't hit me.

Running away is a way to get attention from Silky. I wanted to see if he really cared. He said, "I'm really glad you're back." Maybe that's just what he's supposed to say. But he did say, "For real." You never do know with pimps. Some things

they're supposed to say and some things they say on their own.

This might be becoming a serious relationship, but I'm scared of being swept. If I let myself like him a lot, I would be very jealous and always want him for myself. That's what happened to Linda.

I act nice to Linda. She doesn't bother me, but I don't like her. Linda wants Silky for herself, and she can't have him. Not with me here.

LINDA

I'm still in love with Silky, but I don't like him the way I used to, *Linda admits*. I used to see him every day. Then it was every other day. And now it's every few days. I don't like working seven days a week for nothing. I have Silky, but Silky isn't everything. And I don't have him all the time.

Last weekend, I couldn't reach him for three days. He and Tracey just disappeared. Kitty was at the apartment and said they didn't take any clothes. First I thought something bad had happened to him. Then I got mad.

I finally reached him on Sunday night and I says, "Where've you been for three days?"

He says, "I ran off."

I says, "Ran off where?"

"I just ran off." He's laughing cause he's playing like he's one of his girls.

I says, "Why didn't you call?"

" 'Cause I was afraid you'd beat my ass."

I says, "What?" Now he's really giggling like us.

"I thought you'd beat my ass for running off. I was scared to come back." I couldn't help smiling. Silky can be so charming and funny. But I've gotten to know him and I don't like him as well.

Silky's always been inconsiderate. Like you've been out working all day and night and then you go to jail at three o'clock in the morning. I hate jail, because it's dirty and boring. You don't have any sleep.

At eight o'clock, you get out of jail and go right to Silky's apartment. You have to give him a bath and put lotion on him and massage his back for two hours. Then you cook his food, clean house, run to the drugstore, and pay the phone bill. I'm not a girl who has a pimp so he can order me around. I chose because the life was exciting and I liked Silky. I accept the or-

dering, because that's part of Silky. I enjoy helping him sometimes, because I love him. But I can't do everything all the time.
I'm just a girl.

Silky says the reason I'm not happy is that I'm not making
enough money. He's giving me game. When I first met him, I
thought he liked me for myself. Now I think he likes me for my
money. If I were making more money, he might treat me better. But Sandy makes good money and he treats her lousy.
Sometimes he doesn't see her for a month. Silky feels I'm immature. To him, maturity is being so confident in you, he
doesn't have to be involved any more. That's the way he is with
Sandy.

When I first got with Silky, we didn't have a money relationship. I used to spend whole days with him. Instead of going to
work at night, I'd stay with him. He never said anything about
money when I was doing bad. Sometimes I'd just make fifty
dollars. I wasn't even trying.

Silky's attitude has changed. He says, "The money's going to have to get better." Silky never cops any girls in the winter. Maybe he doesn't like to work in the cold. But Kitty, Sandy, and me were out in the snow for him. We ought to get better treatment for working in thirty degree weather.

Silky is a summertime pimp. He cops his girls in June. His spring attitude is: Start making money or you can leave. He gets new girls and he automatically gets overconfident.

I keep thinking I would have more material things if I was working a straight job. I have nothing. What's a mink coat if you don't have shoes or clothes? Kitty and I don't have any furniture in our apartments. We have bedroom sets, because they're necessary for work. Silky orders drapes and they never come. He says I complain too much, but he never buys me nothing and I've given him thousands and thousands of dollars. What's more, Silky's spending every cent he has on coke. I'm not going to work hard just so he can blow. I may not be getting anything financially out of him—but at least he should save my money. He just spends it on silly things for himself.

I've started running off for a day or two. Two weeks ago, I phoned Silky and he hung up three times 'cause I was laughing and kidding. Then I sent him a card: "Remember when our eyes met. Remember when we kissed?" When you opened the card it said "Remember?" I signed it "Miss X" and came back. Kitty was furious.

I always come back. I can't seem to stay away. I hate Silky the pimp, but I'm still in love with Silky. Life without him is so dull and empty. I don't know what to do with myself.

Tuesday, Kitty and Tracey and me were all at Silky's house and Silky sent me and Kitty downstairs to do some business. We came back in ten minutes. We had the keys to the apartment, but I said, "Let's ring. I don't want to walk in on anything." We rang and no one answered. We waited for fifteen minutes. Finally Silky comes to the door in his bathrobe. His underpants were on the living room table. Tracey was in the bathroom. I said, "You don't have to rub it in my face. I know you do it with other girls."

"I wasn't doing nothing."

"Then what's your pants doing on the table, and why's Tracey in the bathroom?" I just ran off. I went to a hotel and phoned Silky. I gave him the impression I was going to commit suicide. I told him I'd taken sleeping pills—fifteen—and I was going to sleep. He said, "Isn't it kind of dangerous, going to sleep after taking that many pills?"

I said, "Silky, I'm really crazy."

"I'm coming right over. If you have to go to the hospital, I'll take you. Where are you?" I wouldn't tell him. I started to laugh. Then he must have thought I was bluffing, because he hung up the telephone.

I came back. Kitty had run away and come back too. She probably heard that I'd left. Kitty leaves when I'm around and if she thinks I'm going to leave, she comes back. She just doesn't want me around—even though we're friends. She knows Silky prefers me. Kitty would probably never run off if I left for good.

Silky was really mad at both of us for running away. He hit Kitty with a belt and she got bruises all over. Kitty doesn't bruise easily. He beat me up a bit—but only on the face. Then he made both of us get down on the bed. He said we should . . . sixty-nine. He said, "If you have no respect for me, you have no respect for yourselves. Now you go eat each other." We just pretended. I could never do that. I know Kitty has, but she didn't do nothing to me. Silky must have been crazy-angry to even think of making us do that in front of him. He hates it. But he just sent us off to work afterwards.

When we first got together, I'd do anything for Silky. But I can't work seven days a week any more. I think we should have Sundays off. I'm working too hard. I have rings under my eyes. I'm always tired. I'm getting to look like an old hag. I'm working for nothing. I need a vacation. I can't get one. Silky's a lousy employer.

Silky said he would come home with me. But then he decided not to. I think he's afraid of my aunt. Maybe he's embarrassed too. My aunt knows Silky but she doesn't connect him with pimping. She thinks I'm with the Mafia. She sends me every article on white slavery.

In the beginning, I didn't think about myself. I was happy and I just thought about being happy with Silky. This was a love affair. We used to go to square places and Silky paid attention to me. Now when we go out, we go to bars with people in the life. Silky's off flashing with the other guys and trying to cop girls. Once in a while, maybe once an hour, he'll come back to me and make sure I have a drink. Meantime, I'm not supposed to talk to anyone while he's off having fun. I'm alone with him. I don't think Silky's unusual in that. Pimps do it. They look down on women. I don't like pimps. I fell in love with a pimp and I just don't like the life. It's not for me.

I know Silky still cares for me, because I just found out I was pregnant. When I told Silky, he says, "Don't you want to have a little Silky?"

I says, "But Silky, I slipped up on my pills and I don't know whose baby it is."

"Don't be silly, Linda. You can only get pregnant when you come, and you don't come with tricks, right?"

I start laughing. "Where'd you ever hear a silly thing like that?"

Silky's real serious. "I learned it in high school physics."

It turned out that my period was just late and that was lucky. Especially 'cause Kitty was pregnant at the same time. She wanted to have the baby and Silky made her have an abortion. When I told Silky I wasn't pregnant, he said, "That's lucky, 'cause Kitty would have shot me."

If Silky said, "Look Linda, I love you and I know you hate the work, so you don't have to work," then I'd stay. But he'd have to plan some kind of future. Anyway, Silky would never say that. He's too professional. He may still love me a little, but now we have a money involvement.

I want a square relationship that will lead to marriage. I can't go back to a routine life. Working as a secretary, I'd make one fifty a week. Now I make at least a thousand. I'd have to do some soft hooking on the side.

All the square people I meet are pale. You get hooked on this life and nothing else satisfies you. Maybe I'll meet someone I like as much as Silky. If I can ever leave him for good.

SUMMER

LOIS

Lois is staying with me now, *Silky says*. Sometimes she stays with Linda. Lois was with me and Linda drove her away. No use inviting that again. I think Linda is glad she's back. She's glad she got her girl friend here and she's glad she got me another woman. It's almost as important as going to work. A girl is not required to get other girls. But I favor her if she does.

I like Lois sexually. She's even more fragile than Linda, but I don't have time to spend with her. Lois is very quiet. I never know what she's thinking. Our relationship doesn't have depth, but Lois doesn't demand attention. She just needs to belong and I try to give her a sense of belonging.

Our relationship will go someplace whenever I have time to separate her from Linda and make them two individual relationships.

I've been with Silky off and on since Linda's been with him. I come and go, *says Lois*. I've known Linda for a long time. We got turned out in the life together. Linda and I get along good. Some friends you can only stay around for so long and you get sick of them. That's not Linda. What's more, I trust her. If she was going to do something, she would have done it to me already.

I don't lie to Linda about anything, but she lied to me about coming to New York this time. She said she wanted me to come and help her leave Silky. She just couldn't go by herself. But now that I'm here, it's easier for her to stay, because she has a friend and she's not so lonely. I don't think she'll ever go.

I loved the life in the beginning. It was so fancy. I got caught by the glamor—diamonds, cars, furs, and fancy apartments. That's going to catch any girl's eye. I'd never seen it before.

You figure if you go with a pimp, you'll be part of the glamor. They're like movie stars. That's what turns you out and starts you in the life.

When I first went with black pimps, I'd walk down the street and feel proud. I knew I was putting white people down by going with a black man. I felt rebellious. Once you start going with a black man, it's hard to stop. They're different and attractive. There is also a mystery to them. I know white men better than black men. I got fascinated by the difference. The colored race is free and easy. They do what they want to. They just don't give a damn. Meantime, white society cares what everyone else thinks. You'd be surprised how many white guys are trying to pimp. I'd never go with a white pimp—he just tries to duplicate the black man—something that he's not.

When I'm with a white guy, I'm more emotional and let myself go. With a black guy, you have to be careful. If you really get involved, he could let you go and hurt you. Black men are more emotional sexually, but mentally they're cold.

A pimp is a father image. His strictness is what you'd expect from a father—he tells you what to do. A boy friend or a husband would not have the same strictness; he wouldn't say, "If you don't do this, you'll get punished." With a square guy, you have equality and you do what you want to.

Many girls who have pimps come from good families. They've been spoiled and they like to have someone telling them what to do for a change. That's why I'm drawn to a pimp. I was brought up doing what I wanted. I've always been able to make up my own mind. Now I have someone that tells *me* what to do.

You want direction, but at first it's hard to accept. I had never been controlled before. And finally now I have someone swatting me around instead of confusing myself. I feel very female. I couldn't find a square man who was that strong.

I am constantly quiet around Silky. We're all supposed to be. He does let you speak freely—to a certain extent. Until you start giving your opinions. Sometimes he even lets you give your opinion. Silky and I have a funny relationship: it's "hi" and "good-bye." Pimps are accustomed to sweet-talking girls, when they're copping and when they're afraid a girl will leave. If you want to get attention, you can be difficult and get him to sweet-talk you. But I've played that game out. I've been with ten pimps in two years. I don't want to play anymore.

I'm attracted to Silky, but I'm not really swept. I have to be careful all the time, because I could get hurt. He might get mad and put me outside. As long as I continue to give Silky money, I suppose he'll keep me on. That's part of the agreement. Some
180

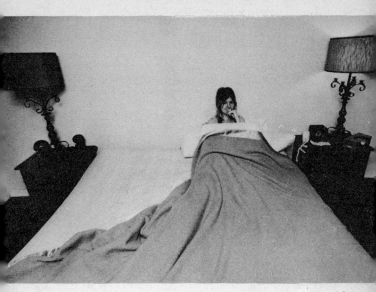

pimps say good-bye and drop you. I don't think Silky would do that.

Linda and I started going out with straight guys. We'd pick up young, hip guys on the street—or they'd pick us up. Then we'd go to square bars and clubs with them. At midnight, we'd say we had to go home, because we had to get up early for work. Little Cinderellas. Then we'd go on to work. We never told these guys what we really did and we never went to bed with them. A couple of guys turned me on, but I feel that sleeping with someone else would be cheating on Silky, so I couldn't do it. But it isn't that I didn't want to.

Silky told Linda when I'm around I never smile and I'm never happy. I'm not. I like to be by myself. Linda said, "Well, she doesn't like you and you don't like her."

He said, "That's true. But I want her money." That's all he wants. You'd think he could get along without my two hundred dollars a day. I thought he was bigger than two hundred dollars. He's so big and mighty.

A pimp is supposed to give you inspiration to make money. Of course, he gives you inspiration so you give money to him! The majority of pimps don't give you nothing. When you start getting older, you've given up all that money for nothing. If I came out with nothing in the end, I'd like to look back and see that I'd spent it on myself.

I don't think Silky would care if I left. Except for Linda, who he loves, all the girls are money in his pocket. That's the way he feels. He can just turn around and cop.

Kitty and Sandy would never leave Silky. But I think Linda might. It would be hard for her to leave. She loves Silky and they have a really close relationship. It would be hard for her to kick him. But Silky's copping every day now and he's too busy to give Linda time. Besides Linda doesn't like the life. I wouldn't want her to spend as many years as Sandy's spent and not get nothing out of it. Which is exactly what's going to happen.

You hear things on the street. Everyone says, "You leave Silky and you get your ass kicked and you have to come back. You have all your clothes taken away." A woman should have the prerogative to stay or not. With Silky, she has no choice.

Silky sure enough won't let Linda go. If I left, he wouldn't let Linda out of his sight, because when I leave, he'll suspect that Linda is going to leave too.

LINDA & LOIS

Linda: I was having a big fight with Silky on the phone. I told him I was leaving. I told him I was unhappy. He said I was tearing down what I'd been building up—what *we'd* been building up. I said, "I'm slowly beginning to not feel the same way about you I felt before. I don't like you."

He always tries to put the blame on you: "If there's any problem, it is your problem, because you're changing. You're not going to be the same girl you were when you came with me." I started screaming and yelling.

He said, "That's the sweetest thing I ever said to you in your whole life. Now get over here."

I thought he was going to beat my ass. I said, "No, I'm not coming."

He said, "You don't appreciate nothing. You don't appreciate me being nice to you. You don't appreciate me putting you in front of everyone else." All that shit. I started yelling and told him I wasn't coming over for him to kick my ass in. So he said, "Get over here anyway."

He thought I was coming and phoned back a couple of minutes later: "Don't bother coming. I ain't going to kick your ass. I just don't care."

Lois: Silky doesn't hide his feelings about you from anyone. He favors you. He can deny it, but he doesn't play it off very well. Oh, he's straight with you in front of his other ladies. But you can't hide your emotions when you care.

Linda: He says he don't.

Lois: I can tell he does.

Linda: No, he's stopped.

Lois: What should I say?

Linda: Nothing. I *know*.

Lois: But *I* can feel it. You just want me to reassure you.

Linda: Don't be silly.

Lois: He loves you. That's what you want to hear.

Linda: But seriously. How can he? He makes me work the streets and I have this warrant on me. How can he love me and put me in jail?

Lois: If he keeps climbing fire escapes, that's where he'll be. He shouldn't just kick down doors. Someone's going to call the cops. And any cop can tell what profession he's in! He wears it.

Linda: Silky told me to keep tipping the doorman—which I do. But the doorman told Silky he couldn't come in here without ringing the bell. Silky just kicked the door and the doorman got scared. But no cops came.

Lois: Silky feels discriminated against as far as color goes. All pimps do.

Linda: Yeah. Silky's got a lot of complexes. He's got a bad inferiority complex. He's always trying to cover it up. He says, "I don't do much, but what I do, I do.well."

Lois: I don't think he feels guilty about being a pimp.

Linda: Not about being a pimp. About his own self. When he talks about girls who've gone away, he says, "They all come back."

Lois: It's true. They all *do* come back.

Linda: But he keeps telling everybody about how good he is. "I can do this and I can do that." He doesn't have any confidence in himself. Sure, he's brainwashing us, but he's also brainwashing himself.

Lois: I don't think he has anything to have a complex about.

Linda: But I don't think he has any confidence in himself. He just uses sex appeal.

Lois: No, sex is for his own personal needs. I think he needs more sex than most people. He must go three or four times a day. That's with different girls.

Linda: I bet Silky has sex with every girl that walks in the door.

Lois: Black. White. Chinese. Yellow. Pink. I've been in the bedroom when he's out in the living room making it.

Linda: I've been on the couch when he's in the bedroom. I don't mind him fucking other girls, but I wish he wouldn't do it when I'm around.

Lois: He just can't help doing it all the time. But I don't think he has one girl friend on the side he sees regularly.

Linda: Neither do I. It's one girl one day and another the next.

Lois: He's just got to satisfy his own needs. He couldn't care less if I come.

Linda: Sometimes he makes me feel like I'm turning a trick. He tells me what to do and I've got to do it whether I feel like it or not.

184

Lois: Yeah. He is sort of like a trick. I give to him, but he's not giving back. I play around with him, but he sure enough isn't going to take the time to play around with me.

Linda: He comes awful fast.

Lois: But when he has coke, he's cool.

Linda: Then he takes a long time.

Lois: But usually he tries to get it over with.

Linda: He jumps in and goes fast. I'm not even aroused.

Lois: And then he just goes off to sleep afterwards.

Linda: He just likes to get off.

Lois: I don't think he cares if I have any pleasure or not. He's not considerate. You have to have sex with him when he tells you to take your hat and coat off. That's the signal. If you don't take your clothes off, he says, "Didn't I give you an order?"

Linda: "Did you hear what I said?" Then he'll be really nasty when he does it.

Lois: That's his routine when he's in the mood to have sex all of a sudden. He says the same thing to everyone. Kitty's told me. Sandy's told me.

Linda: Of course, we're supposed to get satisfaction out of pleasing him.

Lois: That's what he says! Everything's for him.

Linda: When Silky's satisfied, we're satisfied. *Supposedly.* I don't think there's a woman who couldn't please him.

Lois: Not the way he goes about it.

Linda: He's a freak. A position freak.

Lois: Switching all around. He leans over. Standing. Sitting. He throws me around. By now, I could go to bed with him by the book. He's nice though. Personalitywise. He's got a good personality. He can play up to anybody.

Linda: And he's really fun to be with at times.

186

Lois: I just keep wondering if he's going to throw out all the white girls one day.

Linda: He does have this thing about the white man and the black man. He was watching Sammy Davis on TV and saying how Sammy used the white man to get what he wanted. Silky's using white women, but he lives off the white man. He calls himself Jesus. That really gets me. I still have a little religion. He calls himself "Silky Christ." Silky thinks he's God.

Lois: But he doesn't have anything put away. He hopes to have something. Like he'll get Sandy a beauty shop. I'm not impressed by his diamond ring and watch.

Linda: But in the beginning, it used to fascinate me.

Lois: But anybody can get diamonds.

Linda: It's just a game. One pimp is trying to be bigger than another. Silky's ring is badder than someone else's ring. His diamonds larger.

Lois: That's all he's got though. And his clothes. He's got nothing backing him up. No money in the bank.

Linda: If he lost all his girls, he would have absolutely nothing. He'd have to sell his jewelry and his cars. *We're* always capable of making money and he's not always capable of getting it.

Lois: He has to work to get new girls.

Linda: And Silky's becoming really, really lazy. He's been trying to get me to get girls for him. When he went to Montreal last time, he copped Tracey on the very last day. Before that, Silky used to get girls all the time.

Lois: He asked me to call my friends in Ottawa. I said, "Who do you want?" He can't even take care of the girls he has. He doesn't treat me badly. He doesn't treat me at all.

Linda: But he treats Kitty the worst.

Lois: You know, Kitty lies about a lot of things. She says she has a big relationship with Silky and they don't have anything.

Linda: No. Kitty says that sex is all they have. But I don't think they have the best sex. Kitty has animal sex. She has to feel that their sexual relationship is best, because that's all she has. Every time she sees Silky, she fights with him.

Lois: She thinks she's getting affection by making him beat on her.

Linda: Kitty told me if she doesn't see him for a week, at least she's going to see him for a half an hour when he comes over to kick her ass.

Lois: Some girls are like that. Tracey and Kitty both provoke Silky. But Tracey gets more attention than Kitty. You're still the favorite. You get the best of everything. Sandy holds everything to herself. She knows you're the favorite. She does every-

187

thing the right way and doesn't get anything for it. She gets even less of Silky than anyone else.

Linda: Sandy's very phony and two-faced. I worked with her my first night out, and after that, when I'd see her on the street, she wouldn't even say hello. She makes snide remarks. I think she's jealous of me. Silky thinks I'm jealous of her, but I never could be.

Lois: I've heard a lot about Sandy crying to other people about how upset she is, but she never tells Silky. She's upset about the way Silky treats her. Of course, she has very good girl friends. She might be a lesbian. I think she goes both ways.

Linda: But Silky always uses Sandy as a model. She doesn't get hit much. I don't think he hits her at all. She doesn't do anything wrong. That he knows about.

Lois: Silky feels more for you.

Linda: He used to treat me different from everyone. But he doesn't any more. He's losing his feeling.

Lois: He can't feel about someone for a long time. He loses interest.

Linda: He probably feels for a girl for a year or so and that's it.

Lois: There are so many girls around. One girl's his favorite; then the next girl who comes along is his favorite. Who knows who it'll be tomorrow? One day you just find a girl you like better. What's more, she's new and fresh. A challenge. Silky likes to prove he can always get new game.

Linda: In the summertime Silky sees more girls and he's around me less.

Lois: He told me: "Linda's not going anywhere."

Linda: He thinks every once in a while that I'm going to leave. But he thinks if I do, I'll come back. Because I'm in love with him. He doesn't think I'll be leaving any time soon.

Lois: It's funny I've never resented the way he felt about you. I guess I've never been in love with him. I don't feel like falling in love right now. I'm holding back. I like him, but I'm only here because of you.

Linda: But Lois, I'm so, so tired of Silky. I'm on to his game. I don't want to be with other women for the rest of my life. I don't think there's any future in this. If he ever does save up and buy me a business, I just don't want to work. I don't want to run off every time I need a vacation. When my brother or my cousin visits, you know what Silky says? He says we can't afford time off. "Tell them you're going away."

Lois: Working seven days a week and all night is no life, for sure.

Linda: There's never any change. I get depressed so easily now.

188

I definitely don't want another pimp. I'm sick of pimps.

Lois: I think subconsciously the way he treats us is a hatred of white people. It's a way of getting back.

Linda: Do you think Silky prefers black women? They always like their own kind.

Lois: Well, he can't allow himself to relax with us. He can't be tender, because he *is* a pimp.

Linda: I suppose he can't break down the image. You know he got thick with one girl and she gave him a lot of trouble. Maybe he feels that way about me.

Lois: I really prefer square guys. You know they think about you and don't go from one girl to another.

Linda: I like squares because you can be with them as much as you want.

Lois: And there's no fear in a square relationship. Pimps raise their hands fast when they get mad. It's part of the brainwashing. I'm tired of doing what *they* want.

Linda: I can't even say what I want to. I don't feel myself. Silky plays on me and makes me feel good. But that's part of brainwashing. I've begun to realize.

Lois: When I first got with a pimp, I believed him. Then I matched stories with the rest of the girls and realized it was all garbage. But it's a whole new experience for a white girl.

Linda: I feel uncomfortable around black guys. The other night, Silky had some friends over and he made me come down so he'd look good. One fellow said, "You're the life of the party, aren't you?" But I'd been working and I was tired and very uncomfortable.

Lois: Don't you think a black guy feels uncomfortable around all white girls? I can see it in Silky's eyes.

Linda: I don't even want to think about him any more. I'm just really tired. I want to save up some money and quit. I can't be like Sandy. Sandy makes out she's got a lot. She's got plans that include Silky. Plans for little materialistic things that will be coming to her slowly. Like for her anniversary, Silky's ring, and for her birthday, fur hot pants, and for Christmas she wants a white mink coat. Silly little things like that she's going to wait so long for. And work so hard for. Sandy just doesn't want to start over again with another man. And she doesn't want to stay in the life by herself. Sandy was telling me that she never gets to see Silky and she never complains. But Silky's so sure that Sandy's never going to leave that she couldn't even get to him by telling him she's leaving. He wouldn't believe her. He does believe me. Soon I'm going to mean it. Now everything bothers me. Especially Silky.

Lois: This life is so depressing and Silky scares me.

Linda: Pimps try to make you scared all the time so you won't leave them. I would never tell on Silky. I don't think he worries about that. If you told on a pimp, every pimp in town would be after you—ready to kill.

Lois: Tracey did put a case on somebody once. The fellow had beat her up quite badly and she put an assault charge on him. But she didn't say she was giving him her money.

Linda: If Silky ever gave me any kind of trouble, I'd give him trouble. I'd get someone after him. I wouldn't put a death-certificate contract on him, but I know the right people—syndicate people in Vegas who're tricks of mine. I have connections.

Lois: You talk so tough! You'd never do that!

Linda: But I'll never be with a pimp again. I'll probably miss Silky. I'll probably miss pimps. They're so spirited and fun. But I want to forget him. It will be painful for me. But not as painful as if I left when I really liked Silky. Now everything bothers me.

Lois: I wonder if you'll ever go?

It's a hindrance to have Lois around, *Silky says*. Linda and Lois talk. When I go to Linda's, Lois is always there. Now we are three.

Lois: Last night I met a man who sprayed mace on me.

Linda: After a while, I've gotten pretty good at judging who I should go out with. I just don't go with a guy who speaks smart.

Lois: I don't go with a guy who's drunk. But the trouble is that all the guys want to spend now is twenty dollars. That's ten guys to make two hundred. You can't be too selective.

Linda: I always try to get fifty. I'll be waiting around a long time passing up thirties. I'd rather stand on the corner and turn two tricks for a hundred than hustle and get four for twenty-five. I don't spend time with tricks anyway.

Lois: I'm usually pretty nasty. If they don't come when I want them to, they've just got to get out.

Linda: My guys say, "I thought there was no time limit." I say, "There's not. But you can't stay this long because of what you're spending." Whatever they're spending, they can't spend a lot of time. They could spend a hundred dollars and wouldn't get any more time than a twenty-dollar guy.

Let's try to go off with guys together. It's so much easier to party.

Lois: Just remember. No lights on. I have a complex about people watching me. Don't you think tricks have a tendency to keep their eyes open? They just stare at me.

Linda: What I can't stand is kissing. Kissing is so personal. I've had Sandy's dates this summer and they all kiss. I just screw a guy so he can't get that close. It's so intimate when you're kissing. . . . Do pimps try to pick you up?

Lois: Yeah. They know I'm with Silky. They say, "All of Silky's girls look like square girls."

Linda: The only one I'm interested in is Flash. He's very good-looking. I've thought about him. If I went with him, I could really hurt Silky.

Lois: But Silky has that rule against talking to other pimps.

Linda: What about slouching?

Lois: [Obviously quoting Silky] "You're not supposed to

slouch against the wall. You're not supposed to stand next to colored girls."

Linda: One night I was standing with a bunch of black girls and Silky drove by. He says, "Don't you ever let me see you standing next to those greasy creatures again." He's yelled at Kitty for sitting on parked cars.

Lois: But Silky is better than some pimps. He doesn't watch us on the stroll. Just every once in a while he drives by.

Linda: It's the cops I hate. They pick you up for just walking down the street.

Lois: I was in a restaurant for fifteen minutes and the cop came in screaming, "You shouldn't hide in here. Why do you make me come in and drag you out?" I was just eating.

Linda: They do that to me too. They just write it up as a loitering charge—a phony charge. They say, "Refused to account for presence on location," "Has no money on her." Really phony charges. But I can't fight them, because they know I'm a prostitute.

LOIS LEAVES

I chose Silky to help Linda out. We were going to leave together. But I don't think Linda's going to be able to leave. And I can't wait any longer. So I'm going, *Lois says.*

Linda's a good friend, but she can't help me now. If she gets caught by Silky, she'll get in trouble. She crossed him once before. Once before she tried to help me leave and Silky found out. He told her she'd better not cross him again—for me. That what he said. He said he was going to make an example if I tried to leave again.

I'm just trying to think of what he'd do if he caught me. I imagine how black and blue I'd be. And maybe a broken bone. A few cracked ribs. What he did to Tracey was horrible. She provoked him and he really went wild. He beat her and there was blood all over the place. Then he made her wash herself and started slapping her again. He thought he'd keep Linda in her place by doing this. He may not like beating, but he sure does it enough. He said, "The next one who pulls anything like this is going to be an example." I'm the next one to leave. I'm going to be the example. He's probably trying to get Linda to tell him where I'm staying. He'll ask her what name I'm under. If I had a chance to talk to him, I'd tell him exactly why I'm leaving. "Because we have no relationship." Linda told him already and he agreed. Personally, we don't like each other. It wasn't *all* that stone cold. But at times I hate him, because he wants people to feel he's the big one. He's a dirty bastard. He's just out for himself. Materialistic things come first. He puts everything before his ladies. He had enough money to fix his car or get Linda a birthday present. He fixed his car. That hurts a person's feelings.

Basically, he has no understanding. Pimps don't want to understand. They think you should want to do what they say.

They think everything they say is right whether they're right or wrong.

Now Silky's gotten three months out of me. And six thousand dollars. After expenses. I've got some clothes at his place, but that's a loss. I've lost so many clothes through pimps. When you leave a pimp, they take all your clothes and everything else you've got. My mother has bought me more clothes than a pimp ever has. I'm better off with her anyway. Pimps like it when you have parents that help—with clothes *and* money. All pimps give you is sex.

Sometimes I feel I'm becoming very prejudiced against pimps. I just don't get along with niggers. Ninety-nine out of a hundred niggers are pimps. I don't think there's anything inside them. I've been through about ten pimps. One pimp I was with I could talk to. I could tell him what was on my mind. We had a relationship. But I got tired, because we were living in hotels and moving around, so I left him.

Pimps say you're free to leave. But they take all your money and everything. How are you going to leave with no money? No money. No clothes. No nothing. I had to stash some money from Silky so I could go. [Lois phones Silky to say she is leaving.]

I just talked to Silky on the phone. I told him he wasn't going to beat me. I said neither one of us had an understanding with each other. He said, "Why do you leave this way?"

I said, "Because this is the only way I can leave. I ain't no punk." He said he was going to stomp my head.

I said, "No, you're not."

He said, "Never mind. I'll see you before you leave the city." He and Dandy were going to the airport and Dandy was going to cover American and he was going to cover Pan Am. He said I'd never get out of the country. But I'm not going to let him threaten me. Threaten for what? He said he was going to kill me. But how? He was cussing, "Dirty bitch. Dirty bitch. Dirty bitch." He's probably still smarting and cussing. I said enough. He hung up.

I think this whole thing is pretty funny. His frightening and threatening me. Like, where's he going to find me? He's got my mother's telephone number on his phone bill. I'd go crazy if he ever phoned my mother. I don't think he would. I think he's got too much respect for a girl's parents. He wouldn't hurt anybody's parents.

As long as I'm in the life, I could meet up with him. But if he comes to Ottawa, he's not going to do anything to me. I'll guarantee that. I'll have about fifty thousand white guys jump all over him. 'Cause they're having this big battle in Ottawa. They're after the colored guys. One colored guy jumped on a white guy. Now the whole city's against them.

Silky's basically a good man. He doesn't pressure you for money. That's where he's good. But there's very few people he treats right. The only one he treats right is Linda. The understanding between us was pretty shitty. It was warped.

Now I'm nervous, but happy.

LINDA & SILKY

Silky doesn't think I'd ever leave, *says Linda*. He knows I'm involved with him. He thinks I'm so involved, I can't leave. He
tells me I'm his.

After Lois left, he treated me real good. Tracey left too, and
then he was much more attentive. Sex has always been good
with Silky. But now he's started going down on me. He pre-
tends it's his finger, but he's really down there himself. Pimps
aren't supposed to do that.

Silky's acting like he did when we first met. He said he was
going to stop talking about the past, because, if we lived in the
past, we wouldn't have any future. He's been real nice, but he'll
probably change again.

Silky's really gotten into partying now. I was so tired of New
York, he let me go to Washington and stay with his girl, Sherry.
I was working with her off the phone. Silky came down to visit.
He made us get in bed together. Now he's learned how to do it.
He fucks while someone sucks. I don't even like Sherry, so I felt
awful. But I have to do what Silky wants.

First we went to Miami together. Silky was thinking about
me living there. He's been branching out. He's going to have
girls all over the country. Now he has Sherry in Washington
and he's always had one or two ladies in Boston. Someone will
stay in New York.

At first, Miami was a holiday. Silky and me were on the
beach every day. We'd go out boating. Now Silky can't swim
and I can't swim, but we love to boat. So we're out alone in the
middle of the ocean and the boat breaks down. Silky was really, really scared. I've never seen him scared before. I think he
was praying, but not to the pimp god. It was for real this time.

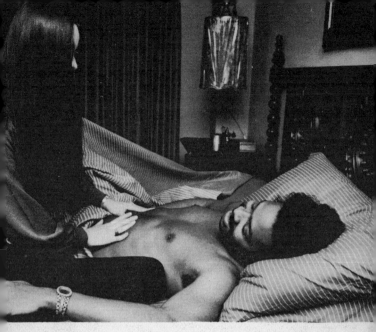

One day, I got mad at Silky, 'cause he was yelling about my money. We'd been having so much fun that I just didn't feel like working. When he started cursing, I ran away and locked myself in my room.

Silky comes to the door and I won't let him in. He's hollering. Then he starts to kick on the door. I went out on my terrace and put one foot over the railing. When he broke in, I jumped into the pool. We both laughed.

Silky had to go back to New York to work. I just couldn't make any money in Miami. So I called him and he sent money for me to come back.

I hadn't given Silky a dime when my aunt came to town. He gave me money to take her out. Then it was my anniversary and Silky bought me a diamond ring. It's the biggest diamond he's ever given anyone. Silky took me to Atlantic City for three days. Stevie Wonder was singing there. He's blind. Someone told Stevie that a young couple were celebrating their first anniversary—us. If Stevie could have seen, he would have known what that meant. Instead, he stopped singing and said, "Let's have a toast to the lovely young couple on their first wedding anniversary." Silky was furious. He wanted to cop girls at the show. That ruined the evening.

I didn't have to work the street. Silky let me work in clubs for a while, because I have a warrant on me that Silky won't take care of. I still didn't make any money. Silky told me he wanted me the way I was and he understood why I didn't make money. He'd accept it, but he couldn't accept me if I didn't try to work.

Then Silky changed his mind. He said I had to go back out on the street—even with the warrant. I've been out on the street for a month and I don't think I've spoken to five guys. I have a new trick who I see all the time. We smoke [grass] and don't have much sex. He's kind of ugly and fat, but he makes me laugh. When I need money to give Silky, I go to him. If he'd keep me, I'd leave Silky and stay in New York. He hasn't asked.

So I just spend my evenings sleeping or at the movies. I won't go out on the street. I'm scared. Silky won't do anything about the warrant. He told me to wait until I get busted and then he'll take care of it. But then I'll have to do time. I'm not going to jail for nobody. Including my pimp. I know I'd go crazy. I go crazy thinking about it. I couldn't handle doing time. Sandy can. Kitty can. Silky's already done time. He's strong. But me—I'd flip out.

I'm still in love with Silky. But I'm not in love with Silky the pimp. It's the pimping business I can't stand. Sending me out on the street is part of pimping. Silky knows how frightened I am. How much can he care for me if he makes me go out? As a pimp, he has to make me. I thought he loved me for me. But basically he's a down pimp and even though he might have gotten carried away with me now and then, he's gotten himself back together as a pimp. That cuts me out—as a person. I don't want to be another one of Silky's ladies.

Now Silky's blaming me, because he says he gave up pimping for me. He isn't copping and he doesn't even pimp the girls he has. He lets all of us get away with murder. Just 'cause he got wrapped up in me.

One day, I went down to his apartment and said I was really leaving. I said I wasn't going to work so hard and I certainly wasn't going to work the streets no more. He said I had to stay because it was my fault. Because he let me sit down, everyone else sat down. He said, "You're responsible for girls leaving and for all the trouble I have with the girls I have. You got me into this and you're going to get me out. You can wait five years for me, bitch." He lost his cool. He was so mad he took it out on the dog.

This morning Silky called and told me to come over to his place. I didn't phone him back. I left and checked into the Holiday Inn. I can't keep on working for a year with nothing more than I came with. I've been wearing the same shoes all summer. That's bad professionally. Silky is under the impression that everything's great unless you complain. When I ask him about shopping, he says, "Next week." And next week, he says next week, and it keeps on going. It's a cloud of promises.

Silky thinks too much of himself. If you love someone, you can't be that selfish. Other guys in the life aren't that way. I've thought of choosing Joe Black. He buys you a phone business and you can keep your apartment if you leave. He lets you spend all the money you want on clothes. Lois was thinking of choosing him too, but she's just been going out with Cau-*ca*-sians. Joe Black might be good till I get settled. I just can't remember what he looks like.

When my mother came to visit, she thought I was doing so bad she took me shopping. That's how Silky takes care of you. I had more clothes when I was square and living with my parents. I haven't been making money in the past few months, but when I was making four hundred dollars a night, I wasn't getting anything anyway.

Linda: I'm spending his money, so I guess I'm really going to go. [Linda returns to hotel and phones Silky at the barber shop to tell him she is leaving.]

Silky: Where've you been all day?

Linda: [Timid] Walking around. Window shopping.

Silky: Didn't you have something to take care of?

Linda: I couldn't. I was busy.

Silky: [Suspicious] Busy? Window shopping?

Linda: [Now defiant] I went shopping.

Silky: You had my money. Did you spend the whole five hundred?

Linda: I only spent one fifty.

Silky: [Authoritative, not realizing Linda has left] You have to return everything. You have to work tonight and get the hundred fifty back and then I'll send you to Ottawa for the weekend. Or you could come to Atlantic City with me. Or you can stay in New York. Or if you want to leave, just leave. No girl can ever get away with taking my money.

Linda: Well, it was our money. Our money. I was the one who gave it to you. Remember?

Silky: You haven't made any money in months. You're just a ho-bo bitch. How do you have the nerve to spend some money I was going to use to get a girl out of jail?

Linda: You've been using money that you should have used to pay off my warrant. I've been having this warrant on me for three months. I've been going out to work every night and thinking about going to jail. You could have used that money to get the warrant off me. But instead you've been spending it on yourself. Right now, I'm just thinking about spending money on myself.

Silky: I'll have to hurt you even though I don't want to. Because you took my money. No girl can ever get away with taking my money. If I don't do something to you, I'll be a chump. You're going to eat your words.

Linda: I don't think you'll be a chump.

Silky: That don't matter. Because you know that I don't ever let a girl get away with that. You put me in a position. I'm coming over.

Linda: Don't bother. I'm not home.

Silky: You have a responsibility. You have a responsibility to get Kitty out of jail. She's in again. I've been running around all the motherfucking morning and all the motherfucking night trying to get the money to get that bitch out of jail. Now I've got the motherfucking money. I want the bitch out of jail.

Linda: I'm not going to do it.

Silky: You know what I'm going to do to you?

Linda: You going to jump on me?

Silky: You know what I'm going to do to you if I find you?

Linda: You aren't going to find me. I'm not going to let you. Are you crazy out of your mind?

Silky: You can't go with my money.

Linda: A hundred dollars ain't nothing. I've given you thousands.

Silky: I'm going to tell your aunt I paid a thousand-dollar bond on you for prostitution and I want it back.

Linda: You know what's going to happen if you tell her that?

204

I'll put a bomb in your motherfucking ass. I'll put a warrant out for your arrest for white slavery.

Silky: You have no right to talk to me that way.

Linda: How about you? Are you going to jump on me and kill me?

Silky: I'm not talking about killing you.

Linda: You are now. Because of the way you're talking. You're crazy if you think you're going to play me into coming back. You're going to jump on me and you know it. But how can you

touch me now? You're having your hair done. Go back and get it done. I ain't staying here. You can't give me another assignment. I've already gone. I've already checked out of your apartment. I can't keep asking you and asking you every day for every little thing I need. You don't do what you say you're going to. You never do what you say. I don't know how you can trust me anyway. I could use the money to make up for a lot of shopping for this year. You could have me. We could have been together. If you would have taken care of things. I'm not playing. For one time, I'm not playing. I've already left.
[Linda hangs up and phones Lois long distance.]

I'm gone. I left him. But he says I'm the only one he can trust to get Kitty out of jail. I'm the only one he can trust with the money. He says this is my last assignment. After I do this, I can leave. I can even take my ring with me. I think he's trying to trick me back. He's giving me game. I said, "You don't have any assignments for me, because I've left you. I've left all my responsibilities. I don't have any responsibilities any more."

He said he was going to kill me. He said he was going to tell my aunt he'd put up a thousand-dollar bond on me for prostitution and he wanted his money back. You know what I told him? "You do that and you're going to have a hundred-thousand-dollar bond on your motherfucking ass." I've never said that to him. I've never ever cursed him before. But if he told my aunt, I would put a case on him.

He kept saying all he wants me to do is get Kitty out of jail. He says he's never tricked me before. He said, "Check the res-

206

ervations in Atlantic City, because I was going to take you there for the weekend. But you can go your own way now. Just get Kitty out of jail." I can't let him talk me into it. I ain't getting Kitty out of jail.

The lawyer could go and get Kitty out of jail. He must be really crazy. He said I owed him this one last assignment. I don't owe him anything. Kitty's not my responsibility. I said, "I'm sick of you. I'm sick of talking to you."

He says, "Wait. No, wait." I says I ain't no ho-bo bitch. 'Cause I was making money and I never had anything.

He says, "You're the only one I can trust to get Kitty out of jail." He says he's going to find me anyplace I am and he'll tear up the town looking for me. He's just mad enough to do it, 'cause I'm paying thirty-five dollars a day for this room. It's the first time I've ever yelled or cussed at him. I'm really going to leave. [Linda phones Silky]

Silky: You've got to get Kitty out of jail.

Linda: Don't scream at me. I'm on my way to the airport. I'm going to miss my plane. And I ain't missing my plane. You ain't going to get a chance to get me. I'm leaving shortly.

Silky: [Gently] What's wrong?

Linda: You know what's wrong. You ain't going to get another chance. You didn't take care of the warrant. You wouldn't take care of the warrant when I cared. Now you think you're not going to have my money, so you talk sweet.

Silky: [Quietly, persuading] Come on back, baby. I need you.

Linda: [Still furious] Stop begging. You never do what you say you're going to. How can you care about me? What can I mean to you? You want to put me out on the street with a warrant on me. I ain't going to jail for no pimp.

Silky: I'll take care of the warrant.

Linda: I don't believe you. You had your chance. You would have let me go to jail. Suppose you didn't have no money for bail. I'd sit there like Kitty always does.

Silky: [Angry] Funky bitch.

Linda: I ain't no funky bitch. I'm not playing on you. I have dropped my responsibilities. You can't make me feel bad. You can't make me take care of your business. I don't feel sorry for you. I don't feel sorry for Kitty. You're not going to get me. You can't talk me out of it this time. I've already gone. What time is it?

Silky: Seven o'clock. You've got to get Kitty out of jail.

Linda: It's too late. She can't get out till morning. Jail closes at seven.

Silky: It's open twenty-four hours.

Linda: The House of Detention. Not Riker's Island. Anyway, I'm not doing it. You can send someone else. You don't have to send me.

Silky: It's your problem. You put me in this position. You owe it to me.

Linda: It's not my problem. I don't owe you nothing. I'll leave your money with the doorman. You can get somebody else to get Kitty out. You know it and I know it. Call one of your ladies!

Silky: No, I can't. Come on.

Linda: I heard you. You're not changing my mind. Even if you were with me right now, you couldn't influence me.

Silky: [Teasing] That's new to me.

Linda: [Angry] New to you? That's what we've already done. Accept the fact that you're wrong. You've been wrong to me.

Silky: I know. I'll take care of you. I've been wrong.

Linda: Saying you're wrong doesn't do anything.

Silky: [Imploring] I'll change.

Linda: [Sarcastic] You're going to change? I don't believe you.

Silky: But I have changed. I've tried to take care of you.

Linda: [Defiant, making him beg] You have not. That's all you're doing—saying it. Mean it. Mean it.

Silky: I do mean it. . . . You're destroying everything we've built.

Linda: You're destroying it. You *have* destroyed it. For yourself.

Silky: I'll do anything for you. You want to go shopping?

Linda: It made me feel better today.

Silky: You can go for a vacation . . .

Linda: . . . and go shopping too?

Silky: Of course. Go shopping

Linda: But you're still going to do something to me. You're going to make me eat my words. That's what you said.

Silky: We'll start again.

Linda: How can we? It's gone. I'm gone.

Silky: I'll take you to Riker's Island. I'll come meet you. Where are you?

Linda: I won't. I don't trust you. Why don't you get a lawyer?

Silky: Meet me at the barber shop.

Linda: I won't come down to Harlem to a barber shop. I don't trust you. You're going to make me go to Riker's Island. Then I'll be back.

Silky: I'll come get you.

Linda: You don't know where I'm at. I'll be leaving in a minute.

Silky: Let's at least talk.

208

Linda: There's no use talking. I'm not sure I can get a plane to-night.
Silky: Where are you?
Linda: I won't help you till I'm sure I can get a flight out tonight. Then I'll get Kitty out and leave.
Silky: I'll come pick you up. Where are you?
Linda: This is the last thing I'll do for you.
Silky: Where are you?
Linda: At the Holiday Inn. I'll meet you downstairs.

Everytime I try to leave Silky and I come back, I'm more involved with him, *Linda reflects*. I thought I couldn't work as a prostitute. I ran away from Silky. I came back and worked. I thought I couldn't walk the street with a warrant on me. I left. But I've come back. I'm walking the streets. I get in deeper with Silky everytime.

I would like for everything to be peaches and roses, *Silky says*, but it can't be and it's not all my fault. When Linda leaves and comes back, we're closer together. But we're also a little more separate.

I resent Linda's leaving. Sometimes it takes a month for me to get back my old feelings. I lose confidence in her. You can say, "I forgive you," but you're still a little hurt.

Each time Linda runs off, she discovers there can be no escape —she's hooked. She runs away to nothing. With me, she has something—me. But I feel that the ball is always on the twenty-yard line. I run to thirty, and she runs off. Then we're back on the twenty again.

I feel that Linda is becoming more serious. She's making the same kind of progress Sandy did. Maybe she's adjusting to the fact that her life is *the* life. But how long will it take her to adjust? She *can* learn. But her teacher's feeling kind of blue.

GLOSSARY

Bad—Good.

Bottom Woman—A pimp's main lady. She has been with him longest, earned privileges and is entrusted with responsibilities.

Chump—A pimp who has just enough money to fulfill his basic needs. Also, more generally, someone who is stupid.

Choose—To select a pimp; a voluntary choice.

Coke—Cocaine; a drug preferred by pimps.

Cop—A pimp induces a girl to choose him.

Crack—To insult in jest.

Dis con—Disorderly conduct; a common charge by police against prostitutes on the street.

Family—A pimp and his women.

Flash—Eye-catching style; a style which attracts prostitutes.

Fly—Good or best; also, a reference to a manner of speech, way of dress and general life style.

Game—A pimp's strategy in dealing with his women; in Silky's case, the "game" is romance.

Get down—Have intercourse; also, to become serious about what one is doing.

He say-She say—A girl talking to another person about her personal business with a pimp.

Ho—Whore, Southern pronunciation, now common usage.

Party—Two girls work on one customer together.

Pimp—A man to whom prostitutes give their earnings.

Player—A pimp or someone in the "life" with style.

Pross—Prostitute.

Square—Straight; outside the "life."

Square up—Get out of the "life" and live in the straight world.

Stroll—Street where prostitutes walk and work.

Sweet—Effeminate.

Sweet Mack—A charming, non-violent pimp.

Swept—Romantically carried away.

The "life"—An underworld community of pimps, prostitutes, hustlers and gangsters.

Trick—John; date; customer.
Turn out—To take a straight girl and make her a prostitute.
Wife—A pimp's woman.
Wife-in-law—The relationship of one pimp's woman to another of his women.
Work—To solicit clients.
Working girl—A prostitute.

Have You Read these Bestsellers from SIGNET?